EDITOR'S LETTER

Songs of defiance

Musicians around the world are refusing to perform their final encores, writes **SARAH DAWOOD**

MUSIC HAS BEEN described as a "cultural universal" – a practice found in all known human cultures and societies. While anthropologists still scratch their heads over exactly where the concept originated, evidence indicates that humans have used musical instruments for an astonishing 40,000 years. During an excavation in 1995 in Slovenia, researchers discovered a bear's femur bone with holes in it and concluded that it could be an ancient flute.

Humans have always found ingenious ways to make music, and it's not difficult to see why. It is one of the most powerful forms of self-expression, capable of eliciting both intense happiness and sadness in the listener. It is used to celebrate, lament, respect and enrage, and its endless genres, styles and instruments form a core part of countries' unique cultural heritages.

But despite its universality, music is being silenced globally. Religious extremism, political factions, racism and nationalism are all driving forces, stopping it being performed, produced and listened to. In this issue we explore how music bans have been weaponised to silence communities and erase histories.

I investigate how, in Afghanistan, musicians have been forced into exile or hiding. The Taliban's "vice and virtue" laws stipulate that consuming music amounts to "moral corruption". They have publicly burnt instruments to demonstrate this ideology, including the national instrument, the *rubab*. Scholars say this amounts to cultural genocide.

But musicians are standing up to their oppressors. Exiled singer Elaha Soroor told me that she writes songs in solidarity with Afghan women who have been stripped of their human rights, including their voices. Assistant editor Katie Dancey-Downs also interviews Iranian singer Golazin Ardestani on how music can be a formidable tool to use against restrictive regimes.

The Ugandan opposition leader, activist and singer Bobi Wine tells Danson Kahyana how he has circumvented the government's bans by hosting concerts in his own home and sharing his music online. "While autocratic regimes use censorship to silence critical voices, sometimes it is that censorship that amplifies our voices," he said.

The Western world is not exempt from musical censorship. As Malu Halasa reports, Black women's voices have been locked out of the US rock movement and typecast into soul and jazz instead. She interviews Felice Rosser, lead singer of FaithNYC, about how she's made her way in a white, male-dominated industry. And on our own shores, editorial assistant Mackenzie Argent explores how drill music is being criminalised by the police, as if the artform itself were an offence.

Elsewhere in this issue, we explore how a new law in Iraq could make journalists' lives harder; the historical censorship of books in Vietnam; and whether Donald Trump's re-election could turn the USA into a "hybrid democracy". We're also excited to publish a series of artworks created by Russian prisoners who oppose the war in Ukraine, and a moving piece by Israeli journalist Dimi Reider on a year of tragedy in Gaza.

Music may not be as essential to life as water, food or safe shelter – but it is at the core of human existence, and has been for millennia. It is a fundamental but also joyful element of free speech. We must defend it – because without it, the world would be muted. ✖

Sarah Dawood is editor at Index

53(04):1/1|DOI:10.1177/03064220241306972

Whistle in the dark

Our cover artist **TATIANA ZELENSKAYA** visualises how music can be a powerful force in the face of adversity

TATIANA ZELENSKAYA WAS born and grew up in Bishkek, the capital of Kyrgyzstan and studied art at the National Academy of Arts of the Kyrgyz Republic.

In March 2020, she was arrested for taking part in a women's rights protest and in 2021, she won the Arts category in the Index Freedom of Expression Awards.

She is currently working on an animation project, exploring the subjective experience of fear and repression. In our cover illustration, she visualises the dual forces of oppression and defiance. Zelenskaya continues to work on other projects as a freelance artist, including animations, illustrations and posters.
You can see more of Tatiana's work at
instagram.com/ tatyanazelenskaia

FRONT COVER CREDIT: Tatiana Zelenskaya

CONTENTS

Up Front

1   **SONGS OF DEFIANCE:**
    SARAH DAWOOD
    How ever much authoritarians try to turn down the volume, musicians will play on

6   **THE INDEX:** MARK STIMPSON
    Moments that matter in the free speech world, from US disinformation to a democracy void in Belarus

Features

12 **ADDING INSULT TO INJURY:**
    NOUR EL DIN ISMAIL
    Turkey is not always welcoming to Syrian journalists

14 **WAITING FOR THE WORST:**
    ALEXANDRA DOMENECH
    A daring few Russian politicians are staying put

17 **SOMALIA'S MUZZLED MEDIA:**
    HINDA ABDI MOHAMOUD
    The challenge of seeking out the truth in the face of daily risks

19 **FURTHER INTO THE INFORMATION VOID:**
    WINTHROP RODGERS
    A new law in Iraq could hinder rather than help journalists

22 **PEACE OF MIND:** CHAN KIN-MAN, JEMIMAH STEINFELD
    From umbrellas, to prison, to freedom. A word from a founder of the Hong Kong Occupy movement

26 **"SHE WILL NOT END UP WELL":** CLEMENCE MANYUKWE
    In Rwanda, opposition politicians have a nasty habit of being assassinated

28 **MODI'S PLANS TO STIFLE THE INTERNET:** SHOAIB DANIYAL
    India's prime minister is keeping a tight grip on what goes online

30 **EDITOR IN EXILE:** IAN WYLIE
    A Burmese journalist shares his story of arrest and escape

32 **EVADING SCRUTINY:**
    BETH CHENG
    China's new tactic for dealing with critics: keep the trials under wraps

34 **LOWERING THE BAR:**
    RUTH GREEN
    Working in law in Afghanistan is now impossible – if you're a woman

37 **A PROMISE IS A PROMISE:**
    AMY BOOTH
    Argentina's president is taking a chainsaw to media freedom

UP FRONT

40 **GOING OFFLINE:**
STEVE KOMARNYCKYJ
Beyoncé is blacklisted in Russia and the question remains: who runs the world?

42 **THE BEACON OF HOPE:**
NILOSREE BISWAS
The next chapter is unwritten for a library in Delhi

44 **A STORY OF FORGOTTEN FICTION:** THIÊN VIÊT
In Vietnam, book censorship is a fact of life

Special Report: Unsung heroes

HOW MUSICIANS ARE RAISING THEIR VOICES AGAINST OPPRESSION

48 **THE SOUND OF SILENCE:**
SARAH DAWOOD
Musicians in Afghanistan fear for their livelihoods, lives and culture

52 **THE WAR ON DRILL:**
MACKENZIE ARGENT
Artistic freedom is not a privilege extended to all musicians

55 **A FORCE FOR GOOD:**
SALIL TRIPATHI
Exploring the soundtrack of resistance in Bangladesh

58 **GEORGIA ON MY MIND:**
JP O'MALLEY
In the face of repression, the beat goes on in the Caucasus

Corrections and clarifications

The following correction relates to Index Vol.53 No.3

P.15 In Nedim Türfent's article, the dance depicted in the photo is not officially banned

CREDIT: Tatiana Zelenskaya

61 **MURDERED FOR MUSIC:**
KAYA GENÇ
The meeting of politics and song can be deadly in Turkey

65 **A BLACK WOMAN WHO DARED TO ROCK:**
MALU HALASA
How one artist smashed into a genre ringfenced for white men

68 **FEAR THE BUTTERFLY:**
KATIE DANCEY-DOWNS
Iranian singer Golazin Ardestani will never take no for an answer

71 **IN TUNE WITH CHANGE:**
TILÉWA KAZEEM
In Nigeria, Afrobeats is about more than a good song

74 **SINGING FOR A REVOLUTION:**
DANSON KAHYANA
Nothing enrages the Ugandan government like hearing Bobi Wine

77 **CUBA CAN'T STOP THE MUSIC:** COCO FUSCO
Government and musicians alike understand the political power of song

Comment

82 **DANGEROUS DOUBLE STANDARDS:** YOUMNA EL SAYED
Israel's closure of Al Jazeera's offices is a warning sign for press freedom

84 **MUSICIAN, HEAL THYSELF:**
MIKE SMITH
The death of Liam Payne brings the issue of mental health into sharp focus

86 **DEMOCRACY, BUT NOT AS WE KNOW IT:** MARTIN BRIGHT
Is the USA stuck in the hinterland between democratic and autocratic?

88 **SILENCE HAS TO BE PERMITTED IN A WORLD WITH FREE SPEECH:**
JEMIMAH STEINFELD
Index's CEO argues that the right to stay quiet is as precious as the right to protest

90 **BIG TECH SHOULDN'T PUNISH WOMEN FOR SEEKING ABORTIONS:**
RAINA LIPSITZ
Trump is incoming. So too is a growing threat to online abortion discussions

Culture

94 **CELL DREAMS: RUSSIA'S PRISONER ART:** MARK STIMPSON
Dissident artwork created under Putin's nose, and shared with Index

99 **NO CATCHER IN THE RYE:**
STEPHEN KOMARNYCKYJ, HRYHORII KOSYNKA
The words of a writer killed by the Soviet regime live on in a new translation

104 **A LIFE IN EXILE:** MACKENZIE ARGENT, JANA PALIASHCHUK
What it means to be homesick, through the eyes of a Belarusian poet

107 **AN UNFATHOMABLE TRAGEDY:** SARAH DAWOOD, DIMI REIDER
One year on from 7 October, a moving piece reflects on the human devastation

110 **YOU ARE NOW FREE:**
ABDELAZIZ BARAKA SAKIN, KATIE DANCEY-DOWNS
An exclusive translation from a Sudanese writer in exile, who has faced ban after ban

112 **PUTIN WILL NOT STOP UNTIL HE'S STOPPED:** EVGENIA KARA-MURZA
The Russian dissident who fought for her husband's release (and won) has the last word

INDEXONCENSORSHIP.ORG

CHIEF EXECUTIVE
Jemimah Steinfeld

EDITOR
Sarah Dawood

ASSISTANT EDITOR
Katie Dancey-Downs

EDITOR-AT-LARGE
Martin Bright

ASSOCIATE EDITOR
Mark Stimpson

ART DIRECTOR
Matthew Hasteley

EDITORIAL ASSISTANT
Mackenzie Argent

SUB EDITORS
Adam Aiken, Tracey Bagshaw, Sally Gimson

CONTRIBUTING EDITORS
Kaya Genç, Emily Couch, Danson Kahyana, Salil Tripathi

HEAD OF POLICY & CAMPAIGNS
Jessica Ní Mhainín

POLICY & CAMPAIGNS OFFICER
Nik Williams

DEVELOPMENT OFFICER
Anna Millward

COMMUNICATIONS & EVENTS MANAGER
Georgia Beeston

CASE COORDINATOR
Daisy Ruddock

DIRECTORS & TRUSTEES
Trevor Phillips (Chair), Kate Maltby (Vice Chair), Anthony Barling, Andrew Franklin, James Goode, Helen Mountfield, Elaine Potter, Mark Stephens, Nick Timothy, Ian Rosenblatt

PATRONS
Margaret Atwood, Simon Callow, Steve Coogan, Brian Eno, Christopher Hird, Jude Kelly, Michael Palin, Matthew Parris, Alexandra Pringle, Gabrielle Rifkind, Sir Tom Stoppard, Lady Sue Woodford Hollick

ADVISORY COMMITTEE
Julian Baggini, Jeff Wasserstrom, Emma Briant, Ariel Dorfman, Michael Foley, Conor Gearty, AC Grayling, Lyndsay Griffiths, William Horsley, Anthony Hudson, Natalia Koliada, Jane Kramer, Jean-Paul Marthoz, Robert McCrum, Rebecca MacKinnon, Beatrice Mtetwa, Julian Petley, Michael Scammell, Kamila Shamsie, Michael Smyth, Tess Woodcraft, Christie Watson

INDEX ON CENSORSHIP | VOL.53 | NO.4

The Index

A round-up of events in the world of free expression from Index's unparalleled network of writers and activists

Edited by
MARK STIMPSON

53(04):4/10|DOI:10.1177/03064220241306581

UP FRONT

PICTURED: In Iran, protester Ahoo Daryaei stripped to her underwear in the grounds of Tehran's Islamic Azad University, in a one-woman protest against the nation's hijab dress code. Pictured here, supporters in London carried out their own similar protests after news emerged that Daryaei was being held at a psychiatric unit. She has since been discharged

The Index

ELECTION WATCH

A new year brings a new wave of elections. Here's who is heading to the polls next

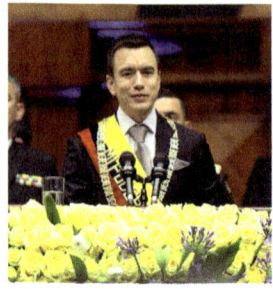

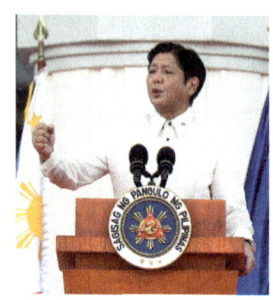

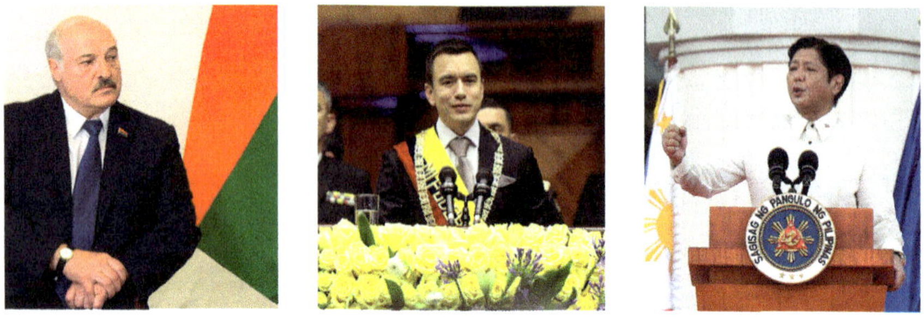

LEFT TO RIGHT: Lukashenka, Noboa and Marcos Jr are all seeking to extend their influence

CREDIT: (Lukashenka) Presidential Executive Office of Russia; (Noboa) Presidencia de la República del Ecuador; (Marcos Jr) Rey Baniquet for Presidential Communications Operations Office; (Navalny) Evgeny Feldman; (Sweeney) handout

1. Belarusian presidential election

26 JANUARY 2025

"Lukashenka has announced the date of his reelection." These were the words of Sviatlana Tsikhanouskaya, the opposition leader who ran against dictator Alyaksandr Lukashenka in the 2020 presidential elections. She ran when her husband, Siarhei Tsikhanouski, was arrested following his announcement that he intended to challenge the incumbent president, alongside many other potential political opponents. The results of the 2020 election are widely reported to have been falsified to guarantee Lukashenka's victory, and mass protests followed, almost leading to the fall of the government. But after a vicious Putin-backed campaign to crush all resistance, his reign continues.

Tsikhanouskaya was forced out of the country under threat of imprisonment, and she established an opposition government from exile. Despite the EU, the UK and the USA all refusing to recognise the results of the last election, it appears that a repeat is on the cards, with fresh reports of hundreds of arrests of supposed dissenters across Belarus in the lead up to the new year.

2. Ecuadorian general election

9 FEBRUARY 2025

Ecuador rushed to schedule its latest general election for early 2025 over fears of increased criminal violence. Organised crime is rife in Ecuador and politicians have been targeted; Fernando Villavicencio, a presidential candidate who ran an anti-corruption campaign during the last election, was murdered by gunmen following an election rally. This was not a one-off incident either – two mayors were murdered in April this year, while two prison directors were killed in September, likely by cartels. These criminal organisations hold great power in Ecuador, and it is expected they will exert further influence over proceedings as they assess which presidential candidate will be best for their interests. Daniel Noboa, who was the youngest president in Ecuadorian history when he was elected in 2023 at just 35, is aiming for reelection amid accusations of American interference. This involved US imposed sanctions and travel bans on former president Rafael Correa, former vice president Jorge Glas, and their families, in what some have seen as an attempt to discredit their former party, Citizen Revolution Movement, which acts as opposition to Noboa's National Democratic Action party. Noboa is staunchly pro-US.

3. Philippine general election

12 MAY 2025

The Philippine midterm general election will see a dramatic clash between two of the nation's most dominant political clans; the Marcos and Duterte families.

All 317 seats in the House of Representatives and 12 of 24 Senate seats are up for grabs. President Ferdinand Marcos Jr is the son of former dictator Ferdinand Marcos Sr, and is looking to consolidate his legacy and influence over his potential successors, midway through his six-year term (presidents cannot run for reelection in the Philippines). He is facing stiff opposition from the Duterte family, once allies: Sara Duterte is vice-president, but stepped down from Marcos's cabinet in July, resigned as secretary of education and has been openly critical of the regime in recent months. Her father, Rodrigo Duterte, was Marcos Jr's predecessor as president, and has announced he is reentering the political sphere by running for mayor of Davao, a Duterte family stronghold, despite being under investigation by the International Criminal Court for crimes against humanity during his presidency. The election is set to be a chaotic affair, and with the Philippines ranking 138 out of 180 in Reporters Without Borders' press freedom index, objective reporting could be under fire. ✖

MY INSPIRATION

Like dancing on a live rail

Journalist **JOHN SWEENEY** was inspired by the late Russian opposition leader **ALEXEI NAVALNY**, who knew better than anyone what standing up to Putin meant

I KNOW, I KNOW, I know. There are a tonne of Ukrainians who point out that Alexei Navalny had a long flirtation with the Russian far-right, that he once sneered at Ukraine's right to Crimea as if it were a "sausage sandwich", and that he never hid his Russian patriotism. He was all these things, and yet he was also the bravest man I have ever met – charismatic, funny, self-deprecating.

And, to be fair, he did walk away from the far-right and never went back; he did say from his gulag punishment cell that Russia must respect the 1991 borders – that is, Crimea belongs to Ukraine; and he told Russia on 24 February 2022 that the war had been started "by the Kremlin gang to make it easier for them to steal. They are killing so they can thieve".

Navalny's contempt for the Soviet mindset was forged in 1986 when the Chernobyl nuclear catastrophe irradiated everywhere around it, including the home of his beloved Ukrainian grandpa and grandma. First, gramps and grandma were told to carry on planting potatoes, that there was nothing to worry about. Then, as the radioactivity alarm bells went off in the West, they had to leave. Immediately.

Navalny understood that a country that covered up design faults in the nuclear power reactors deserved to die. Vladimir Putin never grasped that and believes, to this day, that the Soviet Union was betrayed by traitors controlled by Western intelligence agencies. Putin lives inside this nightmare.

Navalny was no fool. He understood better than anyone else in Russia or abroad that standing up to the Kremlin was like dancing on a live rail. He had had his arm nearly broken, was locked up on moronically contrived charges, was half-blinded in one eye and then was poisoned with Novichok. He recovered but said "no" to Davos and Aspen and to writing op-eds for The Guardian, and he got on a plane back to Russia, daring his enemy to kill him. Like von Stauffenberg standing up to Hitler in Nazi Germany, Navalny stood for a different version of his country: "Another, beautiful Russia."

The ending, we know. ✖

John Sweeney's Murder In The Gulag: How Putin Poisoned Navalny is published by Headline

ABOVE: Alexei Navalny pictured on a Moscow street after he was attacked by assailants with a green dye in 2017

Free speech in numbers

312

The number of electoral college votes won by Donald Trump, who will be inaugurated as the 47th president of the USA this January

1 MILLION

New users who signed up to social platform Bluesky within 24 hours of the US election result

5½

Years in prison that 68-year-old paediatrician Nadezhda Buyanova has been sentenced to in Russia after commenting on the Ukraine war to one of her patients

19,000

People prosecuted in Russia for speaking out against the war, according to human rights organisation OVD-Info

60 billion

Roubles the Russian government plans to invest in its internet censorship platform TSPU over the next five years

The Index

PEOPLE WATCH

MACKENZIE ARGENT highlights the stories of human rights defenders under attack

Marcelo Pérez
MEXICO

Father Marcelo Pérez, a human rights defender and a Tzotzil priest – an Indigenous Maya people who reside in Chiapas, southern Mexico – was killed following a mass on 20 October. He was an ally of the religious Indigenous Movement, which strives for protection of the collective rights of Indigenous people. Father Marcelo led pilgrimages and protest marches, campaigned against drug trafficking and violence, which is rife in the state of Chiapas, and fought for better lives for Indigenous people.

Mansoor al-Muhareb
KUWAIT

In May, Kuwait dissolved its electoral parliament for up to four years, and the Emir, Sheikh Meshaal al-Ahmad, now has legislative power and is targeting those who speak out against him. One such person is Mansoor al-Muhareb, an online activist and blogger who has been sentenced in absentia to two years in prison with hard labour for stating that dissolving parliament was unconstitutional. Al-Muhareb posts online about Kuwait to raise awareness of the repressive policies imposed by the regime on its people.

He Fangmei
CHINA

Health and women's rights activist He Fangmei, who has been in detention since 1 October 2020 after being arrested during a protest, was sentenced to five years and six months in prison, while her family have also been punished. She is an advocate for vaccine safety and access to remedies for defective vaccines. She began campaigning when her daughter was paralysed after receiving a defective vaccine at just 10 months old. Following her initial detention, her infant son was sent into foster care and her two daughters have disappeared.

Gubad Ibadoghlu
AZERBAIJAN

Prominent environmental, human rights and anti-corruption advocate Gubad Ibadoghlu is being denied access to the urgent, life-saving healthcare he requires as a result of his detention and house arrest by the Azerbaijani government when he returned from exile overseas in 2023. Ibadoghlu was detained over false charges brought about in an attempt to silence him and discredit his anti-corruption work and his efforts to provide access to higher education for young Azerbaijanis abroad, particularly in the UK.

Ink spot

Iranian cartoonist and illustrator Mana Neyestani, son of the well-known Iranian poet Manouchehr Neyestani, trained as an architect in Tehran, but then worked as a cartoonist for many cultural, political, literary and economic magazines. In 2006, he was sent to jail because of a cartoon he had drawn which featured in the government-run publication Iran which showed a young boy trying to have a conversation with a cockroach. The cartoon sparked riots among ethnic Azeris in the country who viewed it as a slur on their people, which Neyestani denied. The government closed the newspaper and jailed Neyestani and its managing editor. Neyestani subsequently won Cartoonists Rights Network International's Award for Courage in Editorial Cartooning.

On his release from jail, Neyestani moved to Malaysia and he now lives in exile in Paris.

Neyestani drew the illustration here for the winner of the Trustee Award in Index's 2024 Freedom of Expression Awards, the Russian anti-war activist Evgenia Kara-Murza.

UP FRONT

World In Focus: Georgia

Georgia has faced a tumultuous year, culminating in the Russia-backed Georgian Dream party claiming a landslide victory in the general election, despite exit polls showing a heavy defeat. It's the latest display of corruption in the country

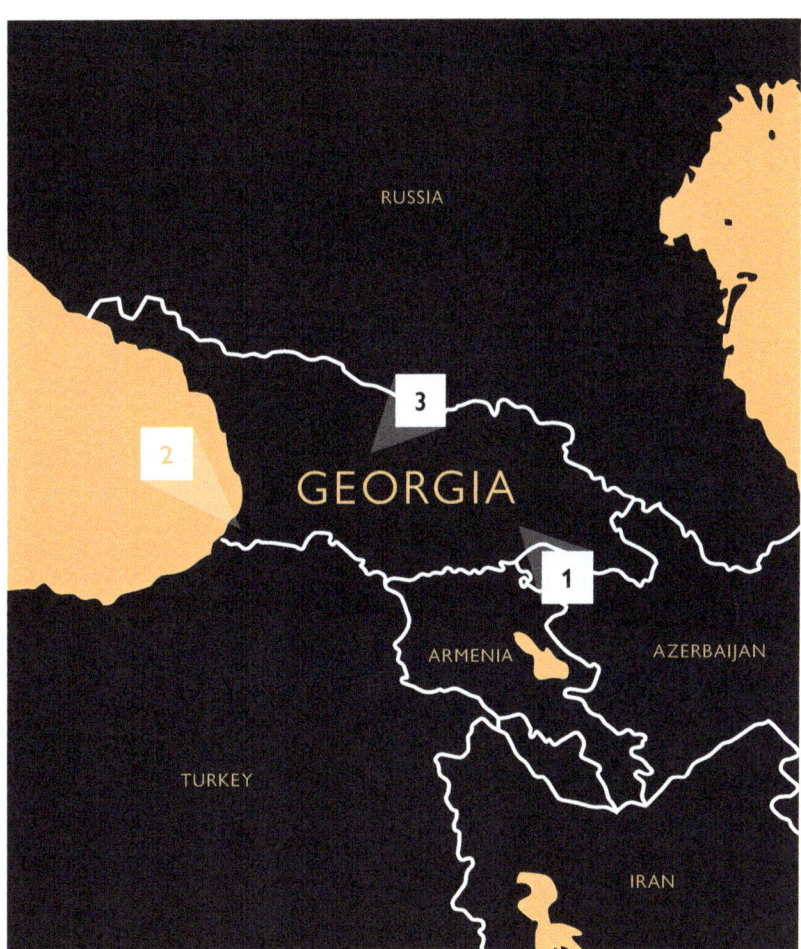

1 Tbilisi
Protests erupted across Tbilisi over the results of October's general election. Widespread reports of voter suppression, ballot-stuffing and violence at polling stations paint a picture of tampering with the democratic process. The streets of the capital filled with citizens waving Georgian and European Union flags. Opposition politicians pledged support for the demonstrations, with some boycotting parliament until their demands for transparency and a new election are met. President Salome Zourabichvili, who is not affiliated with the Georgian Dream party, encouraged the protests and has urged Western governments to denounce the election results and support the protests. Riot police have been deployed to control the protests, and following violent clashes between police and demonstrators in April, tensions are palpable.

2 Batumi
In June, popular British trip-hop group Massive Attack cancelled their performance in the coastal city of Batumi over concerns about human rights violations in Georgia. The decision came after the passing of the "foreign agents" bill, which classifies civil society groups such as media organisations and NGOs as "pursuing the interests of a foreign power" if they get 20% of their funding from abroad – echoing similar legislation in Russia. Georgian Dream passed the bill, citing dangers such as "LGBT propaganda". The bill has blocked Georgia's candidacy for EU membership, which sparked further protests across the country. Massive Attack weren't the only group to cancel a performance in Georgia on these grounds; Georgian band Mgzavrebi cancelled their gig in Tbilisi, instead calling for fans to attend a pro-European protest on the same day, while electronic music festival 4GB was scrapped in protest over the bill.

3 Shukruti
The small village of Shukruti has been fighting to be heard for years. Located in central Georgia near the city of Chiatura, the settlement has suffered severe damage from the work of mining company Georgian Manganese. Residents claim houses have been destroyed, soil and plots have been damaged beyond repair, and local wells have dried up. They reported unbearable living conditions, and after months of protest ignored by the government, some residents resorted to going on a hunger strike on the steps of parliament. Beginning on 1 September, they refused all forms of sustenance bar water, with four villagers allegedly going as far as sewing their mouths shut. Day and night they starved, and 43 days later, the mining company finally agreed to enter negotiations over compensation for the destruction it has caused to Shukruti. Protests will continue until an agreement is reached, but there is hope that the villagers may finally see justice.

The Index

TECH WATCH

The US election, disinformation and truth engines

MARK STIMPSON speaks to documentary director **FRIEDRICH MOSER** on the role of tech in elections

"OVER MY CAREER I have seen an erosion of ethics that was increasingly worrying by the leadership of the United States. Lying has now become acceptable in many countries in the political system, in the financial system and [has] spread. I think we are now in a situation where whole populations are being manipulated into believing something."

These words are spoken by Peter Cochrane, a visiting professor on sentient systems research at the University of Hertfordshire at the beginning of a new documentary. It has been directed by Friedrich Moser and executive produced by George Clooney.

"I don't think people understand the value of truth. I don't think they understand the actual capability of lies to destroy civilisation," adds Cochrane.

The documentary, How to Build a Truth Engine, looks at the rise of misinformation and disinformation and the spread of conspiracy theories. The documentary looks at the Stop the Steal campaign that led up to the 6 January 2021 attacks on the US Congress and the role of QAnon, as well as the Covid cover-up in China and chemical weapon attacks in Syria, which were denied by President Bashar al-Assad.

In the documentary, Zahra Aghajan, a neuroscience professor at the University of California Los Angeles, says: "Conspiracy theories mostly play on fear so once you engage the fear circuitry that memory is there to stay."

Harvard faculty associate and Dangerous Speech Project founder Susan Benesch, who also features in the film, asks "how and why have we come to a point in which we can believe such totally different versions of reality?"

Moser first came into contact with technology that might be able to distinguish the truth from fake news in 2017 while filming his documentary The Maze – Hunting Terror on the Web. He met Cochrane, former chief technology officer of British Telecom in 2019, and identified him as one of the protagonists for a new documentary. Cochrane suggested the documentary's title.

Now, with Donald Trump returning to the White House, I asked Moser about his feelings on the role of disinformation in the election results.

"Disinformation and fake news played a significant role in the outcome of the 2024 US elections, but so have the cost of living and outright racism and misogyny," he said.

But what about the role of X?

"Musk deliberately chose to remove all guardrails against disinformation and conspiracy theories, turning it into a disinformation tool. My take on social media is – and this is true for all platforms – that they are media and therefore need to be held accountable the same way traditional media is. Everybody is free to say what they want. But everybody needs to face the same consequences for falsehoods that traditional media and publishers face."

Moser is sanguine about the role of technology and its impact on elections.

"The media ecosystem has evolved many times since humans started to communicate. Each time a new media tool was added to the arsenal, a shake-up of society ensued. The Berlin Wall would not have fallen, if not for TV soap operas bringing Western abundance into the world of scarcity of Communist economic failures. Obama was the first politician to thrive on the new forms of direct communication of the internet. And Trump was the first Western politician to make full use of social media."

"It's a way too simple excuse to just blame the internet or social media," said Moser. "Disinformation strategies play directly into a weakness of the human mind and the human psyche, and have always done that." ✖

How to Build a Truth Engine had its UK premiere at Leeds International Film Festival www.truthengine.net

LEFT: Friedrich Moser's documentary looks at why conspiracy theories take hold and why they have real-world effects

FEATURES

"As the Taliban filled the Ministry of Justice and the courts with its own lawyers, judges and prosecutors, Maryam's chances of a legal career vanished"

LOWERING THE BAR | RUTH GREEN | P.34

Adding insult to injury

NOUR EL DIN ISMAIL speaks to Syrian journalists who once put their faith in Turkey but are now being arrested for causing offence

IN MARCH 2023, Syrian journalist Ahmed al-Rihawi hosted a Turkish political analyst on his Orient TV show to discuss the killing of Syrians on the Syrian-Turkish border.

The guest, who was angry that his country was being accused of killing people, grabbed al-Rihawi's papers from his hands and tore them up. Al-Rihawi asked him to leave the studio, so the guest threatened him live on air, telling him: "You are expelling me in my country."

A few hours later, a police patrol arrived to arrest al-Rihawi – and his life turned upside down.

Al-Rihawi, who presented the Details programme on Orient TV, and the channel's editor-in-chief, Alaa Farhat, were taken away. They were released 48 hours later, but their freedom was not to last.

At the end of November, Orient – a Syrian platform which had been broadcasting from Turkey and was owned by entrepreneur Ghassan Aboud – closed, leaving dozens of journalists without work.

Farhat wrote on its website that the platform had been under "severe pressures" and that its journalists had "paid a heavy price in terms of their freedom".

A month after the closure, al-Rihawi and Farhat were sentenced to more than six years in prison on charges of spreading hate against the Turkish state and false news. The two journalists fled to Greece.

CREDIT: Mohamad Saeed/SOPA Images/ZUMA Wire/Alamy Live News

PICTURED: Turkish soldiers stand guard during a patrol in a demilitarised zone on the Syrian border, where Syrian journalists have raised questions about deaths at the hands of Turkey

Al-Rihawi told Index that he saw the decision as unjust, recalling the dangers of the journey and the fear that their escape would be discovered.

"The reason for my arrest was that the topic of the killing of Syrians on the border with Turkey was raised for discussion in an episode of my programme."

He noted that he was subjected to harassment during his stay in Turkey and described how the journalists' lawyer attended the sentencing with "all the evidence of the truthfulness of our publication of the news and our journalistic credibility", but it was ignored.

Over the course of 14 years of broadcasting about events in Syria, Orient TV gained great popularity. However, a number of its journalists were arrested in Turkey, including Majed Shamaa, who was held in 2021 following a satirical report he prepared in Istanbul which authorities considered an insult to the Turkish people. He was imprisoned for days and due to be deported before he was released.

Journalist Qusay Amama told Index that he moved to Egypt after he was detained in Turkey while trying to cross into Europe. He said he was working on material about violations that Syrians are subjected to in Turkey at the hands of other Syrians, Turks and people of other nationalities. However, due to the closure of the media outlet he had worked for, he decided to leave the country.

"In April 2024, a Syrian woman contacted me, talking about a great injustice that had been done to her son [he had been given a long-term prison sentence] and she asked me to raise her case in the media," he said. "After I raised it, I was accused of incitement against the state, which I had not really done."

He explained that he was forbidden from leaving Turkey and at any moment he could be imprisoned, and then deported to Syria.

He decided to head to Greece but was stopped by Turkish authorities, who took him to a deportation centre. After hiring a lawyer, he was able to travel on a visa to Iraqi Kurdistan, and then to Cairo.

This summer, military police arrested several journalists in an area of Aleppo on the Turkish/Syrian border which is administratively controlled by Turkey. They included Bakr al-Kassem, a Syrian freelance journalist who worked for outlets including the Turkish news agency Anadolu, and who was released after one week. Karam Kellieh, a member

> Al-Rihawi and Farhat were sentenced to more than six years in prison on charges of spreading hate against the Turkish state and false news

of the Syrian Media Union, was detained for months before being released. Yassin Abu Raed, the founder of Kozal, which covers Syrian news in Turkey, was released after two weeks. The journalists have not spoken about the circumstances and reasons for their arrests.

In 2011, when anti-government protests swept across Syria as part of the wider Arab Spring movement and the Syrian Civil War loomed, Turkey became a safe country for Syrian journalists who opposed the Syrian regime and other factions in the country. Dozens of media outlets, including newspapers, magazines, and radio and television stations, were opened and Syrian journalists formed professional bodies and institutions in Gaziantep and Istanbul.

However, this golden age has diminished in recent years amid unprecedented restrictions. Dozens of journalists have fled to Europe, some seeking asylum.

Amidst an unknown future for Syrian journalists in Turkey, there are limited options. The most likely path for many is reaching Europe so that they can finally report objectively. ✖

Nour El Din Ismail, which is a pseudonym, is a Syrian journalist

Waiting for the worst

ALEXANDRA DOMENECH speaks to opposition politicians who are risking it all to stay in Russia

"MY CHOICE IS made: I'm staying here with the people who need someone to represent their voice," Lev Shlosberg from the Yabloko opposition party told independent media outlet Zhivoy Gvozd on 3 October 2024. This was the day after security forces armed with sledgehammers raided his home in the city of Pskov, as well as that of his 95-year-old father.

Two weeks later, the local Yabloko office was targeted as well. Shlosberg is now facing criminal charges for allegedly failing to disclose his status as a foreign agent, the label he was given for speaking out against the war in Ukraine. People blacklisted as foreign agents by the Kremlin are subject to restrictions on their public activities and have many "duties", such as providing reports for the authorities on what they are doing.

Shlosberg is not the only Yabloko member to be prosecuted: five of its members have had criminal charges brought against them for criticising the invasion. And one of them, Mikhail Afanasyev, has already been sentenced to five and a half years in prison for "spreading false information" about the Russian military.

One independent politician, who spoke with Index from Russia and requested anonymity, said war was not the only topic it is unsafe to raise. Talking about any important social or political issue can lead to punishment.

One area which concerns her is the backlash against women's rights. She is concerned that the state is using blatant propaganda to persuade the public, namely school children, that "a woman's sole purpose in life is to reproduce… because the government needs [new] people".

A new bill, which was signed into law in November, has banned "propaganda" about childfree lifestyles and could lead to the persecution of politicians who raise awareness about threats to women's reproductive rights.

"As a politician, I am aware that [when I speak out for women's rights] I have to control myself more [than before the invasion]," she said, explaining there is other draconian legislation which can be used to punish people "if [the authorities] feel like it".

Gender-based violence is also on the rise, she told Index, a result of the government failing to help veterans from the war in Ukraine adapt to civilian life.

Yulia Galyamina is another opposition politician who has not fled Russia. At the beginning of the war, she was sentenced to a month in prison for calling on people to protest against President Vladimir Putin's aggression.

FEATURES

LEFT: Yekaterina Duntsova enters Russia's Central Election Committee in 2023 to submit her documents as a presidential candidate for the upcoming presidential election

In her last word to the court, she said: "I am a Russian patriot and I believe that sooner or later, our country will become a land of humanity."

Shortly thereafter, Galyamina was deemed to be a foreign agent – and so was the women-led movement for nonviolent action, Myagkaya Sila (Soft Power), of which she is a founding member.

Galyamina believes that politics start with grassroots movements. "Unity of the people, in any form, is political action", she wrote on Telegram in October 2024, arguing that "it is precisely why independent initiatives receive such a violent reaction from the security forces: they see these as a threat to their power".

She was referring to the recent persecution of doctors whose homes were raided by police. They had been supporting their imprisoned colleagues, and had signed an open letter demanding an investigation into the suspicious death of opposition leader Alexei Navalny in prison. Several were detained.

The authorities do not even tolerate initiatives providing humanitarian aid to people in regions near the border with Ukraine, who have been forced from their homes because of the fighting. One such movement, Sograzhdane (Fellow Citizens), was declared a foreign agent. In the city of Yekaterinburg, in west-central Russia, four volunteers, including a minor, were arrested for helping the homeless and charged for taking part in an unauthorised meeting.

Despite the Kremlin's iron grip, people are still capable of mass political mobilisation in support of alternative presidential candidates, even though, since the invasion of Ukraine, the oppression of the Kremlin's opponents, and especially politicians, has been unprecedented.

Dozens of politicians have had to flee the country to avoid being imprisoned. In April 2022, municipal deputy Alexei Gorinov was sentenced to seven years in jail for speaking up about Ukrainian children killed in Putin's war.

Yet at the end of 2023, Yekaterina Duntsova, a little-known journalist from the city of Rzhev, declared her intention to run for president in the national election in March 2024. She said she stood for "peaceful politics" and "democratic values". A month later, she had amassed more than 300,000 supporters on her Telegram channel, but was disqualified from running due to what the authorities claimed were errors in her documentation.

Duntsova urged her followers to support another prominent pro-peace candidate, Boris Nadezhdin, whose last name is significant: *nadezhda* is Russian for "hope". People travelled from remote areas in order to give signatures of support at campaign offices in cities all over Russia, so that he could register as a candidate. Many stood in line in freezing cold temperatures. Nadezhdin delivered 105,000 signatures to the Election Committee – which was more than the required minimum. He too was barred from the presidential elections, for alleged "invalid" signatures.

These efforts were not in vain. People who oppose Putin's politics realised from these actions that they were far from alone and there were others around the country who supported peaceful democratic politics. Dmitriy Kisiev, a politician who created *Shtab Kandidatov* (Candidates' Headquarters), the team which stood behind Nadezhdin's campaign, spoke to Index from Moscow. He stressed that his team "managed to find a way for the people to interact with each other, and with Nadezhdin, in a context [of repression] where it seemed that there was no such opportunity".

"I think that getting the public involved in politics in such dark times is a great achievement," he said, and highlighted that today in Russia "people are often afraid to even say the very word 'politics'".

As for Duntsova, when she wasn't allowed to run for the presidency, she created a party called *Rassvet* (Dawn), which submitted documents for registration at the beginning of November 2024. By the end of →

CREDIT: Alexander Zemlianichenko/Associated Press/Alamy

 People are often afraid to even say the very word 'politics'

INDEXONCENSORSHIP.ORG 15

→ the month, their application had been rejected. She told Index that "independent political activity today is without doubt restricted, as well as the possibilities of people who consider themselves as part of opposition".

She and her team "are very cautious" now, and ensure their activities "have nothing to do with real political action, which could be perceived as some sort of protest".

Instead, they are involved in social activities, supporting political prisoners, organising neighbourhood cleanups and holding discussions and debates – "anything that allows the people to grow into active and thinking citizens".

Despite these seemingly small actions, Duntsova and her party are increasingly under pressure. Rassvet meetings have been targeted by police on more than one occasion. And in October, one of its members, Alexander Germizin, was reportedly detained under extremism charges for comments made on social media.

Another of Duntsova's supporters, Vasiliy Gorelikov, who also worked as a volunteer for Boris Nadezhdin, now faces criminal charges for alleged "extremism on the internet". During the raid on Gorelikov's home, police confiscated letters to political prisoners. Many of Nadezhdin's other volunteers were arrested, in particular those who attempted to do exit polls work during the rigged elections.

Duntsova told Index that she is "well aware of the risks" of staying in Russia, adding that "being labelled as a foreign agent is the least [frightening] thing that could have happened" to her. She recognised that she is "constantly waiting" for the authorities to put an end to her activity, or "for something even worse" to happen.

Nevertheless, she said: "I'm not going anywhere, because my home is here. So, [me and my team] just keep on living and carry on with our work. Whatever will be, will be."

On 29 October 2024, a few weeks after she spoke with Index, Duntsova

She is "constantly waiting" for the authorities to put an end to her activity, or "for something even worse" to happen

was fined 30,000 rubles (just over $300) for, absurdly, "not denouncing herself" as a foreign agent.

Asked by Index whether he fears persecution, Kisiev said that he was "very surprised" that his home was not targeted. He had already been arrested in the past and his home raided for taking part in street protests.

"Maybe [the police] will come [to my home again], but I try not to think about things that I cannot control," he said. "We have learned to overcome our fear."

On the bright side for Kisiev, he believes the public puts more trust in Russian politicians who are persecuted by the authorities.

"Because if someone risks their life and freedom to make [other people's] lives better, it means that they are genuinely devoted to their cause – and must be supported," he explained.

Despite the pressure, Kisiev hopes that one day a citizens' movement for a democratic Russia could be built, "so that the energy and the people, who came together during [Nadezhdin's campaign] could be mobilised to create a positive legal force".

Shlosberg from the Yabloko party remains hopeful, too. In the interview with Zhivoy Gvozd, he said that he stands with "the millions, not just thousands, of people, who need different politics, different treatment, different laws and a different government".

He added: "There is a light at the end of the tunnel – let's just say it is rather far away." ✖

Alexandra Domenech is a Moscow-born, Paris-based journalist specialising in women's rights in Russia

BELOW: Yulia Galyamina was detained after holding a one-person protest during the Covid-19 lockdown in 2020

FEATURES

Somalia's muzzled media

HINDA ABDI MOHAMOUD reports from Mogadishu on the growing pressures that are stopping journalists from breaking stories

SOMALIA IS ONE of the most dangerous countries in which to be a journalist. Reporters don't just face the risk of being caught up in the violence they cover – they are sometimes the targets of that violence or find themselves stuck in the middle of competing armed groups, where keeping one side happy risks angering another.

This is the situation Mohamed Ibrahim Osman Bulbul, a freelance journalist and advocate for media freedom in Somalia, found himself in after a recent government directive regarding Islamist group Al-Shabaab.

"[The directive] stipulated how Al-Shabaab should be named in the media," Bulbul told Index. "We should no longer refer to them as 'Al-Shabaab' but instead as 'terrorists'."

For Somali journalists, adopting this terminology poses serious dangers, especially as there is no one to guarantee their security. These risks force many journalists to focus on international issues rather than critical local stories as they feel they lack the freedom to report honestly on domestic matters.

They also face arbitrary arrest and detention – something Bulbul has experienced. In August 2023, he reported on a case of corruption involving high-ranking police officials. Shortly afterwards, he was arrested.

"In broad daylight, unknown individuals kidnapped me while I was at university," he said. "They [showed] no warrant and didn't explain the reason for my arrest until seven days later."

After being held in an underground cell, Bulbul was transferred to another prison, where he remained for 56 days.

It wasn't the first time his reporting had attracted revenge. In 2019, he reported on Al-Shabaab halting the construction of Mogadishu Stadium over demands for payment. He said the story drew threats not only from Al-Shabaab but also from the government and businesspeople involved in the project. Due to escalating threats, he left the country for a year.

The situation is no better in the towns outside Mogadishu, where there is sometimes even less freedom. In Kismayo, several hundred kilometres south of the capital, there has been no independent media for 13 years. Journalists cannot report on anything that the local government does not approve of, and they also face threats from Al-Shabaab →

CREDIT: Imago / Alamy

LEFT: A video journalist works at the site of an explosion in Mogadishu in 2017. Danger and threats of violence are an occupational hazard for journalists in Somalia

Sometimes the competition to report first can add further risk

→ if the group objects to any stories.

Two months ago, Abdimajiid Abbas Adan, a 30-year-old journalist working in Kismayo, was contacted directly by Al-Shabaab after he covered an attack on a local military base. Before that, he had questioned budget allocations released by the Ministry of Finance in the state of Jubaland and was threatened by the government.

"During the election campaigns [in] October 2024, I reported on one candidate which led to my arrest," he told Index. "After three days, I was deported from my own city, with a one-way ticket to Mogadishu and no explanation given. I have three children and a family in Kismayo, but I don't know when I'll be able to return. My future feels uncertain."

One of Somalia's few women journalists, Maryan Abdiqani has a long list of daily harassments and obstacles that stand in the way of her reporting.

"Reporting on sensitive topics like clan conflicts, terrorist attacks and corruption exposes journalists to threats from all sides, and sometimes the competition to report first can add further risk, as speed can compromise both safety and accuracy," she said.

And she believes that economic interests are leading to oppression.

"I went to report on fishermen protesting [against] the takeover of their fish market by outside parties. My cameraman and I arrived, filmed the news and captured the story," she said.

"But the police intervened, took us to the station and told us we couldn't publish. We were detained for three hours and they deleted all the footage we had recorded."

As well as threats of violence and arrest, journalists face an uphill struggle to navigate bureaucratic hurdles, limited transparency, restrictions on movement and a lack of formal channels through which they can request information. Public offices and private organisations operate under a culture of secrecy, making the collection of reliable data exceedingly difficult.

Hassan Istiila is a freelance journalist based in Mogadishu who knows these hurdles all too well.

"One of the main challenges we face as local journalists in Somalia is gaining access to information," he said. "For instance, obtaining information from the government and the private sector is extremely difficult."

He said there were many reasons for this, the most significant being the security concerns which limit journalists' ability to move freely and prohibit their ability to gather information.

"Additionally, the political situation in Somalia is unstable and sensitive, especially regarding interactions between the federal government and the federal member states. On top of that, private companies have become increasingly reluctant to share information," he said.

Istiila also decries a lack of unity among media associations, seeing this as a major issue. As a result, local journalists often distrust one another and struggle to collaborate. Without a united front they lose their collective influence and cannot advocate effectively for better access to information.

This lack of access has serious consequences. When journalists cannot obtain reliable information, it inevitably leads to the spread of misinformation and unverified news. This erodes public trust in the media and undermines accountability, damaging democratic governance and allowing corruption to thrive.

Farah Omar Nur, secretary general of the Federation of Somali Journalists (FESOJ), regularly hears these issues raised by fellow media workers.

"Journalists often struggle to obtain accurate information, which sometimes forces them to include their personal opinions in their reports," he said. "Government entities, along with public and private organisations, are unwilling to share information freely. They release details selectively – based on their own interests – which makes it nearly impossible for journalists to gather the facts they need. This lack of transparency seriously undermines the fact-checking process and the public's right to receive truthful information."

The FESOJ's latest Press Freedom Report, covering the period from May 2023 to May 2024, documented 28 instances of abuse against journalists, with three deaths. One of those was the result of long-term injuries that a journalist sustained several years ago, when they were the victim of a car bombing.

The FESOJ also reports that 20 journalists were detained during that year while one was tortured and another kidnapped.

"Under these circumstances, journalists are understandably afraid to cover sensitive topics," said Nur. "And when journalists do attempt to report on these issues they frequently face harassment from the police. Although there is a media law signed by former president Mohamed Abdullahi Farmaajo, it has not been actively enforced to protect journalists."

It's not surprising that many journalists are intimidated into silence or, if they do manage to report on controversial issues, are locked up or beaten into silence.

It doesn't look as though this will change anytime soon and Somalia is likely to remain one of the most dangerous places to carry out this most important of jobs. ✖

Hinda Abdi Mohamoud is the chief editor of Bilan, Somalia's first all-women media house

53(04):17/18|DOI:10.1177/03064220241306585

Further into the information void

Journalists in Iraq might soon have a new challenge on their hands, writes **WINTHROP RODGERS**

IRAQ'S PARLIAMENT IS considering a new Access to Information law. In a country where corruption is rampant, such a move might appear a positive development that could help journalists, activists and citizens obtain a clear view of how their government works.

Yet many who have been campaigning for such a law for years are deeply disappointed because the draft proposed by Prime Minister Mohammed Shia' al-Sudani's government does precisely the opposite.

"The government's draft law on the right to access information is deeply flawed and undermines the fundamental principle of information accessibility," Dlovan Barwari, an Iraqi investigative journalist, told Index.

Instead of bringing Iraq in line with international standards around freedom of expression, the law will make it even more difficult for journalists to expose abuses.

A narrowing space

Iraq is a very difficult place for journalists and activists to operate. The 2005 constitution contains formal protections for freedom of expression and the press, but in reality there are many legal loopholes, and people with powerful interests enjoy impunity when they commit violations.

Reporters Without Borders (RSF) ranked the country 169 out of 180 on its 2024 World Press Freedom Index, which represented a drop of two spots from the previous year. Harassment, violence and spurious prosecutions are common.

"Following the fall of the regime in 2003, a period of long-standing repression gave way to new-found openness," Barwari said. "However, this freedom was soon compromised as armed groups and militias began to target journalists, making Iraq one of the most perilous countries for media professionals."

Some people that the regime doesn't like face threats to their physical safety. Several high-profile journalists, analysts and activists have been killed in recent years. Others have hurdles put in their way by the authorities which limit their ability to report what is happening.

"Access to government data is crucial for my reporting," Barwari said. "Government institutions can be unpredictable in their willingness to share information. Any employee may refuse to disclose crucial details, even those that seem straightforward."

He continued: "This situation creates a substantial obstacle for journalists, who struggle to publish anything as a verified, indisputable fact," adding that this allows rumours and disinformation to run rampant.

People in Iraq who wanted to improve the situation for journalists, activists and ordinary citizens believed for years that some kind of access to information law, enforced by the authorities, would be the solution in forcing the government to be more transparent.

Since 2017, Dhikra Sarsam said that her Baghdad-based organisation, Burj Babel for Media Development, has been pushing for such legislation. Working with lawyers and a Danish NGO, they prepared a draft law and submitted it to the relevant parliamentary committee for consideration.

Burj Babel also conducted a survey of 450 journalists about how they worked. It found that 80% of respondents did not get information for their work from an original source. Instead, they relied on social media, unverified leaked documents, or other unofficial informants.

"This is the main thing. It reflects the importance of such a law because we do not have a source to get the information, especially related to ministries and their budgets," Sarsam said.

Despite their advocacy, parliament ignored Burj Babel's draft for years, and then last year, the government came up with its own access to information law which was a complete distortion of what Burj Babel was proposing. The law has already received the first and second of three required readings for passage.

Iraqi civil society and MPs are still working hard to introduce changes to bring the proposed new law up to international standards, but it's now late in the legislative process for revisions and they face an uphill struggle.

Falling short of international standards

According to analysis by human rights group Article 19, the government's draft legislation is littered with problems. The legislation doesn't adhere to any principle of maximum disclosure, where only extreme circumstances should prevent information held by public bodies →

This situation creates a substantial obstacle for journalists, who struggle to publish anything as a verified, indisputable fact

from being disclosed. Nor does the law contain a right to appeal against refusals. Where there are exceptions, Article 19 say they are "vaguely and broadly formulated".

This approach means that ministries will not be forced to disclose information that concerns national security, international relations, commercial interests or privacy. The section in the government's draft which prohibits information being released on how Iraq's federal government handles bids and auction contracts is particularly pernicious, and would make it impossible for journalists, activists and ordinary citizens to lift the lid on the already widespread abuses in government contracting. Iraq has a major corruption problem, ranking near the bottom of global coalition Transparency International's Corruption Perceptions Index. It is common for huge sums of money to be awarded to politically-affiliated companies with little oversight.

Troublingly, the government draft also includes criminal penalties of a one-year imprisonment and a fine for anyone who disseminates a document exempted under the law. People and organisations can also be prosecuted if they provide incorrect information or disclose information regarding national or economic security, with no protections for whistleblowers.

This is only a sampling of the problems in the government's version. Article 19 called for much of the law to be "completely redrafted" in order to comply with international standards.

Burj Babel launched a petition campaign to push MPs to make changes, which was signed by over 900 people, who were largely journalists and lawyers. They are also using other methods of persuasion, for instance, suggesting that Iraq's processes are way behind those of their neighbours. The government's new law says journalists and others have to submit hard copy requests for information and wait for an answer, a deliberately long and cumbersome process. Why shouldn't they be able to do so digitally?

"During our meetings with the parliament members, we show them samples of what [systems are] used in other countries in the region, like Tunisia, Jordan and Egypt, where one can submit electronically to receive the information," Sarsam said.

The government's draft has not yet achieved final passage, meaning that there is still time to change the language before a vote by the full parliament.

Fighting back

Omed Mohammed was a Baghdad-based reporter for Kurdish television channel NRT for years. He covered some of the biggest stories in Iraq from the frontlines of the war against Islamic State and was in Tahrir Square interviewing protesters right from the beginning of the anti-government Tishreen Movement in 2019.

In Iraq's 2021 parliamentary elections, he ran for a seat in his hometown of Kirkuk. He caused upset when he took a remarkable win over candidates backed by more established and larger parties. Because of his past work as a reporter, he strongly supports passing legislation to make it easier to get information from the government.

"We think this law is very important for Iraq right now, but there are many obstacles to it, for it reveals a lot of corruption in Iraq," Mohammed told Index. "The purpose of this law is to

make the government be transparent [for the benefit of] all civilians, journalists and the international community too."

He is confident that changes will be made to the legislation during discussions in the Culture and Media Committee. He told Index that redrafting is underway, which was confirmed by civil society groups that are making suggestions to the committee.

Mohammed's biggest concern was that the revised legislation will not pass when, and if, it comes up for a vote.

Iraqi politics is a delicate balancing act between vested interests. If any of the

 **It is common for huge sums of money to be awarded to politically-affiliated companies with little oversight**

ABOVE: Iraqi Prime Minister Mohammed Shia' al-Sudani, shown here speaking at the UN General Assembly in 2024, has been accused of shutting out journalists to protect the country's image on the world stage

largest parties within the Shia, Sunni or Kurdish ethnic blocs opposes a piece of legislation, it is unlikely to come to the floor for a vote. Mohammed predicted that this would be the case for an improved Access to Information law.

He saw its introduction by the government as a bad faith attempt to burnish Iraq's image on the international stage. By introducing legislation, even one that was so patently against the spirit of transparency, Baghdad is able to claim that it is trying its best to respond to calls from UN bodies and foreign governments to plug this hole in its legal regime.

"But the reality is that the representatives of Sudani's government are against passing this law," Mohammed said.

With a number of other legislative priorities and new elections expected next year, it is not clear when the Iraqi parliament might move forward with the law, and in what form. Barwari said he was heartened by the work of civil society and the reception their suggestions are getting from the committee.

However, his optimism came with a caution: "This cooperation does not necessarily signify the intentions of the political forces within parliament, which tend to prioritise silencing dissent and curtailing freedoms." ✘

Winthrop Rodgers is a journalist and analyst focused on Iraq and the Kurdistan Region

Peace of mind

CHAN KIN-MAN, one of the founders of Hong Kong's Occupy movement, talks to Index CEO **JEMIMAH STEINFELD** about walking freedom's long road

"PRISON WAS TOUGH, but I don't regret a single moment," Hong Kong professor Chan Kin-man told his friends after he left Pik Uk prison in March 2020. He had served 326 days there, having been charged with inciting and conspiring to cause public nuisance for his leading role in the 2014 pro-democracy Umbrella Movement.

Chan's reflections on his time in prison and his fight for democratic rights within Hong Kong and China are collected in an anthology made up of letters he wrote from jail (some of which were published in the now-closed Apple Daily, a Chinese-language newspaper in Hong Kong) alongside essays. Index has published an extract here.

His sense of resourcefulness is pronounced. He speaks about how he frequently read, exercised, wrote and even taught whilst in prison. It's clear that this helped him emotionally. But what also gave him hope during this incomprehensibly hard time?

The story of Taiwan's democratisation was "particularly inspiring", Chan told Index.

"Many of the democracy fighters who were tortured and imprisoned in 1979 lived to see martial law lifted in the late 1980s and the first presidential election in 1996," he said. "Although many others who were killed during the White Terror period didn't witness the triumph of democracy, they exemplified what human values truly mean. These courageous forerunners on the long road to freedom gave me hope."

Chan's relationship with human rights was cemented when he started college in 1979, when the region was at a crossroads.

In China, it was the year of the Democracy Wall Movement, when intellectuals displayed posters in Beijing to protest against social injustices and demand democracy and free speech. In Taiwan, 10 December 1979 saw the arrest of many opposition leaders for organising a march on International Human Rights Day. In Hong Kong, there was uncertainty about the future and whether it would stay under the UK's control. Conversations around the rule of law and freedoms intensified.

Chan said: "These debates deeply affected me, and I increasingly envisioned my vocation as fighting for democracy in Hong Kong and China."

He later studied at Yale, where he met professor Juan J Linz, who was studying the democratisation of Spain. Linz had a big influence on Chan and was one reason he became a scholar.

When he returned to Hong Kong in 1992 Chan had a bold, very admirable mission – to bring civil society to China. Through working with NGOs and foundations, publishing many works, teaching at the Chinese University of Hong Kong, →

> China is a global superpower that may not easily yield to external pressure

RIGHT: Demonstrators at a protest in Manchester against the crackdown in Hong Kong

Extract from Suffering and Resistance: Chan Kin-man's Letters from the Prison

New Taipei: 2022

THE FIRST LETTER my daughter sent me after I went to prison included a famous quote by Dale Carnegie: "Two men looked out from prison bars. One saw the mud, the other saw stars."

As with Gandhi, Mandela, Martin Luther King Jr, Havel, Bonhoeffer, Kim Dae-jung, Malcolm X and others who fought for democracy and justice, imprisonment is a process of solidifying one's beliefs, precipitating one's thoughts and tempering one's mind and body. At Pik Uk, I ran more than 600 kilometres around the ball court. In my spare time, I hungrily read 50 books. My appendix "Reading Against Anxiety: A Reading List for Prison" describes the significance of reading in prison and some thoughts I shared after reading. I read for myself, but I also saw the needs of other inmates. Some inmates said I was a genuine JP (Justice of the Peace) who could seek redress for their grievances. But I must admit that I wasn't as selfless as Shiu Ka-chun, who continued to fight for prisoners' rights in and outside prison. I wanted my time in prison to pass peacefully, so I decided to provide only personal services to inmates. The first thing I did was teach English to some Hong Kong inmates three nights a week, starting with practical vocabulary and conversation, and then teaching some grammar. The students had to talk to foreign inmates and then report back, and I assigned them essays and tests. I acted as a ghostwriter for mainland inmates (usually illegal labourers) reporting their safety to their families, and helped foreign inmates write letters to various government departments. I also helped compile information and write pleas for leniency for prisoners applying for parole. As time went on, other prisoners treated me as a respected elder by helping me at work and avoiding smoking near me.

Most of the prison staff at Pik Uk were very friendly to me. On my first day, when I was about to enter a room for newcomer orientation, one of the staff whispered that I should add an extra layer of clothing to avoid catching a chill from the air conditioning, and the masters in the workshop were always teaching me carpentry skills. Many of the staff called me "professor" in private, often encouraged me to "cheer up", and reminded me to add blankets or clothing. I would talk to them about current affairs and even their children's schooling. Occasionally, a staff member would quietly tell me about the rampant police brutality outside, or would say: "When I take off my uniform, I'm also a Hongkonger!" Even staff members who said they didn't share my political stance still respected me for "paying up" (honouring my commitment) without complaint.

No matter how difficult these days were, the letters I received every day lifted my spirits. There was a "diversion factory" that sent news and online postings related to the protests to inmates to help us keep a finger on the pulse of society. My family, students and many members of the public faithfully wrote letters asking after my welfare, and I often teared up as I sat in a corner of the workshop reading them over and over again. My wife tirelessly travelled long distances every week to visit me and bring books and other daily necessities. Because the visiting time was so short, I was obliged to turn down visits by many well-intentioned friends. Many legislators and lawyers, on the other hand, looked in on me while at the prison on official business and told me about the changes taking place outside, and I will never forget it.

Taking refuge in calm waters

Sixteen months after my release from prison, I finally boarded a flight for Taipei on 19 July 2021. Why did it take me this long, when I'd spent my imprisonment longing to leave Hong Kong for a place where I could breathe freely?

While in prison, I'd read the historical novel Zeng Guofan, which describes how, in his middle years, this great Qing dynasty statesman was advised by someone he admired "not to think in terms of shaking the earth, but to take refuge in calm waters", and this expressed my own mindset. I'd devoted half my life to building civil society in China and fighting for

→ and involving himself in the city's democratic movements, he stayed true to the mission. Even behind bars his commitment to peaceful, democratic change was exemplary.

After leaving prison he spent some time in Hong Kong before moving to Taiwan as a visiting professor at the National Chengchi University, which has become a destination for many fleeing persecution in Hong Kong. He is encouraged to see the proliferation of overseas civil society organisations which fight for freedoms from afar.

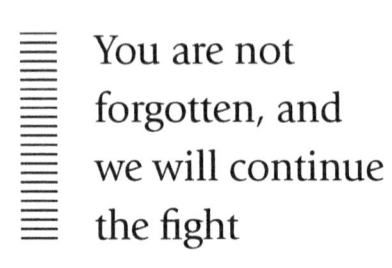

"This overseas protest movement has succeeded in making Hong Kong's story globally visible and raising awareness of China's threat among Western democracies," he said. "It has also helped urge the passage of the Hong Kong Human Rights and Democracy Act in the US Congress."

Activists have their work cut out for them, though.

"China is a global superpower that may not easily yield to external pressure," he said. "External pressure can only provide political opportunities to intensify internal strife within the Chinese Communist Party. Ultimately, the most fundamental struggle lies within China and Hong Kong."

What he misses most about Hong Kong are his friends – most of whom are either in jail or in exile.

"I miss the times when we could march together in the streets of Hong Kong, demanding democracy," he said.

And to those still in prison, Chan has a message: "You are not forgotten, and we will continue the fight." ✖

Jemimah Steinfeld is CEO at Index

> You are not forgotten, and we will continue the fight

democratic elections in Hong Kong, but the former was crumbling, and the latter was nowhere in sight. These aspirations had landed me in prison, and although I was at peace with it, I was also physically and mentally exhausted and longed for a calm and tranquil refuge.

The trilogy A Century's Pursuit describes how when Chiang Kai-shek retreated to Taiwan after being defeated by Mao's Communist forces on the mainland, he tried to stabilise the local situation by winning over the gentry. On multiple occasions he sent people to Japan to persuade Lin Hsien-tang to return to Taiwan, but Lin replied: "The sages teach us not to enter a country in turmoil or reside in a country in chaos." We should keep in mind that Lin Hsien-tang had given his all for Taiwan. Under Japanese rule, Lin had spent enormous sums of money every year on a campaign to establish a democratically-elected parliament in Taiwan, and he supported the Taiwan Cultural Association in an effort to educate the public and fight for self-governance through publishing and lectures. He was part of a delegation representing Taiwan in the ceremony for Japan's surrender to China in Nanjing, but eventually topped the list of traitors in the February 28 Incident. Utterly disillusioned with the Kuomintang government, he preferred to die in a foreign land rather than enter a country in turmoil.

Reading this story in prison, I sighed at how Hong Kong had become just such a land in turmoil. On 14 March 2020 (my sentence automatically reduced by one-third for good behaviour), I stepped out of Pik Uk Prison and told my waiting friends: "Prison was tough, but I don't regret a single moment." Benny Tai had told me there were many things for me to take up outside prison, but I was haunted by the ghosts of Zeng Guofan and Lin Hsien-Tang.

When I returned home to my family, I felt surrounded by goodness and light and relished every bite of food. My plan was to take a short break and then seriously consider accepting an invitation from Professor Chiang Min-hsiu to serve as a visiting professor at Taiwan's National Chengchi University. Instead, returning to a city demoralised by setbacks to a popular movement against the Extradition Law Amendment Bill (hereafter Anti-ELAB Movement), I felt reluctant to abandon Hong Kong, and even felt that I should stick with it through thick and thin.

From a small prison to a big prison
Hong Kong had become an enormous prison. I saw Chinese University's Bridge No. 2 (the site of a battle between police and students during the Anti-ELAB Movement) surrounded by the same razor-wire fence as prisons, police stations and key government buildings, encircled by water barricades, and police officers constantly checking people's identity cards on the street or in subway stations. After the National Security Law came into effect on 1 July 2020, the White Terror spread swiftly. Scholar friends began receiving notices from publishers terminating contracts for books related to the Anti-ELAB Movement, and the publisher of the Hong Kong edition of this book decided to suspend its business. Then, in August, the National Security officers arrested Lai Chee-ying [Jimmy Lai] and his family, senior executives at Lai's newspaper, Apple Daily, and Agnes Chow of the pro-democracy political organisation Demosisto. In January 2021, a large number of pro-democracy activists were arrested on charges of conspiracy to commit subversion for participating in a primary election organised by the democratic camp. In quick succession, other pro-democracy activists were arrested for speech crimes or for raising funds in support of exiled protesters, and panic spread throughout Hong Kong. The National Security police typically arrested people in their homes at 6am, and some of my friends in the pan-democratic camp and media told me that whenever they heard a sound outside their door early in the morning, they thought their time had come. Who can sleep peacefully under tyranny?
Translated by **Stacy Mosher**

PICTURED:
Pro-democracy campaigner Chan Kin-man

"She will not end up well"

CLEMENCE MANYUKWE speaks to a Rwandan opposition leader stuck in political limbo while those around her go missing

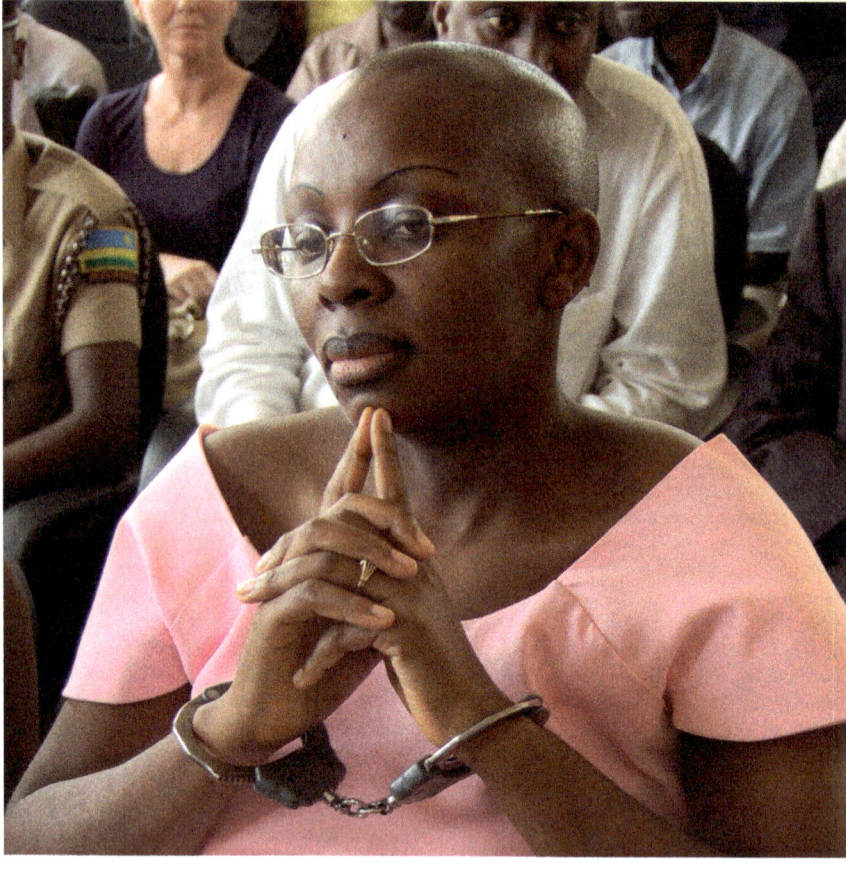

ABOVE: Rwandan opposition leader Victoire Ingabire listens to the judge during her trial in Kigali, Rwanda in September 2011

RWANDA'S OPPOSITION LEADER, Victoire Ingabire Umuhoza, has been blocked from leaving her country since 2018 and barred from challenging President Paul Kagame in elections since 2010.

Some of her aides and supporters have been assassinated. Others have mysteriously disappeared.

Ingabire's troubles started in 2010 when she returned to Rwanda from exile in the Netherlands to run for president. After returning home, she was charged with six offences including "genocide ideology" – for highlighting that Hutus, as well as Tutsis, were subject to mass killings and harm in Rwanda – and "terrorist acts", accused of creating an armed group.

The politician denied all the charges but was convicted and sentenced to 15 years in prison. She was pardoned by Kagame in 2018 after spending eight years in jail, five of them in solitary confinement.

After her release, Ingabire went on to form the Dalfa-Umurinzi (Development and Liberty for All) party, which the authorities declined to register. In 2021, eight members were arrested after taking part in an online training session on non-violent resistance, and they have remained incarcerated for more than two years without being tried.

Ingabire told Index about the fate of some of her other supporters.

"Venant Abayisenga was 30 years old and an orphan. He was my close aide. In June 2020, he left my house to buy some credit for his phone and has not been seen or heard from since. His two siblings still wonder what happened to their brother," she said.

There are others who have been killed, including her regional political representative Jean Damascene Habarugira.

"He went missing in [May] 2017 after openly opposing the government's agricultural planning policies. A few days later, his family members were called to collect his badly-mutilated body from a local hospital," Ingabire said.

She also spoke about her assistant, Anselme Mutuyimana: "He was kidnapped from a bus station in the Western Province in March 2019," she said. "A day later, his body was found in a forest close to his parents' home. He was only 30 years old."

The grim list continues with father-of-two Syldio Dusabumuremyi, who was the national co-ordinator of her political party.

"Two unidentified men stabbed him to death as he worked in the shop of a health centre in the Southern Province. His children still do not know who killed their father or why."

Kagame has ruled the country (first as vice president, when he was widely

> His children still do not know who killed their father or why

considered as a de facto leader) since the end of Rwanda's genocide in 1994, when extremists within the majority Hutu population killed more than 800,000 civilians, primarily Tutsi but also moderate Hutus.

Each election that cemented his rule faced fierce criticism from the international community amid persecution of dissenters – allegations Kagame's regime denies.

Before her arrest, Ingabire – who is a Hutu – had said that for Rwanda to experience true reconciliation there needed to be a recognition not only of the genocide perpetrated against the Tutsi but also of the crimes against humanity committed against the Hutu. Kagame's Tutsi-dominated government deemed that opinion to be a crime of minimising the genocide.

"My opinion was in line with the conclusion in the report of the United Nations, published in December 1994, which highlights evidence of grave violations of international humanitarian law committed in the territory of Rwanda by both parties involved in the war," Ingabire said.

The judicial arm of the African Union, the African Court on Human and Peoples' Rights, found that imprisoning Ingabire had violated her right to free expression. It ordered Rwanda to pay Ingabire more than 66 million Rwandan francs (nearly $50,000). Ian Edwards, her UK-based lawyer, told Index this money had not been paid.

He said the violations against Ingabire formed part of a pattern to restrict political competition. This is part of maintaining the Kagame-led Rwandan Patriotic Front's hold on power.

He said denying Ingabire the opportunity to participate in the democratic process limited not only her own rights but also those of the electorate, which contradicts the principles of a democratic society.

"It also undermines the rule of law by indicating judicial partiality or lack of independence, and shows that legal or judicial processes are being manipulated or interfered with to serve political ends," he said.

Edwards said Rwanda's Criminal Procedure Law states that any person "sentenced to a penalty" can be "rehabilitated". This rehabilitation extinguishes a conviction and all its consequences. The Rwandan courts have turned down Ingabire's rehabilitation application – a refusal that Edwards claims is politically motivated.

He took Ingabire's case to the East African Court of Justice in April but it is yet to make a determination.

Edwards said that Rwanda's government had a long history of stifling any meaningful political opposition, and his client's life was at risk there.

He accused Kagame of making defamatory and inflammatory comments about her during this year's election campaign, including saying: "You know she will not end up well."

He pointed to another threat in July, when a social media influencer told his followers that Ingabire "should count herself lucky that I am not among those

ABOVE: Rwanda's President Paul Kagame casts his vote in a presidential election in July 2024, from which Ingabire was barred from standing

Legal processes are being manipulated

who take decisions on what to do with her. I would suggest that she deserves a bullet in the head".

Ingabire told Index that one of the conditions of the presidential pardon is for her to obtain consent from the minister of justice if she wants to travel outside Rwanda. Once a month, she is required to appear before a prosecutor to confirm that she is still in the country, and she will be doing so until August 2025, when her initial 15-year sentence is supposed to expire.

Since 2019, she has petitioned the minister of justice on four occasions to be granted permission to leave the country and has even written to Kagame. She has had confirmation that her requests and letters were received, but neither has responded.

"As a result, I have been unable to travel to Sweden to attend my son's wedding or to assist with the births of my grandchildren in Sweden and Holland," she said.

She last saw her husband, who is also a Rwandan national, at the airport in the Netherlands on the day she caught a flight back home in 2010.

"Today, I am unable to travel to see my severely ill husband in the Netherlands. Overall, I have been denied the opportunity to enjoy a family life."

In her lawyer's words, this prevention of spending time with her ill husband is incompatible with the basic right requiring respect for family life.

He says it is "motivated by the imperative of keeping her removed from political life". ✖

Clemence Manyukwe is a freelance journalist based in Zimbabwe

LEFT: Prime Minister Narendra Modi at Hansa Dwar, Parliament House in November this year. The current status of a new bill aiming to regulate broadcasters and content creators is unknown

Modi's plans to stifle the internet

The Indian government may have withdrawn its latest plans for a new broadcasting law, but the prime minister still intends to bring his online critics to heel, writes **SHOAIB DANIYAL**

ON 1 APRIL, less than a month before India went to the polls, a young YouTuber named Dhruv Rathee released a video calling India's Hindu nationalist prime minister a dictator. Speaking in a loud, declamatory style, Rathee delivered fact after fact, laying out how Narendra Modi had tried to throttle Indian democracy. The video ended with an appeal to vote against the prime minister.

At the time of writing, Rathee's haranguing had garnered more than 37 million views on YouTube. And this does not take into account the many Indians who would have viewed it as a "forward" on WhatsApp.

With 25.9 million subscribers, Rathee is one of those who Indians increasingly turn to when they want to consume current affairs.

Another is Ravish Kumar, one of India's most well-known journalists, who now broadcasts on YouTube and has more than 12 million subscribers.

These one-person channels frequently attract more views and subscribers than corporate-funded mainstream media channels.

For a decade, India's mainstream media has stopped doing the job it's meant to do – holding the powerful to account. Using a mixture of carrot and stick, Modi has ensured his government has little to fear from traditional broadcasters or newspapers, and the result is that Indians are now increasingly turning to the internet for news and opinion. This trend is so significant that Modi is making increasingly desperate attempts to control what takes place online.

Throttling the press
As a wave of autocratic strongmen sweeps the world, Modi arguably leads the pack. The power he commands and the ideological changes he has made to his country have few parallels, either globally or in India's own history. The tactical keystone of this politics? Control over the country's media.

In 2014, the country's Congress-led liberal coalition crashed to a defeat, bringing Modi to power. This loss was portended by loud television debates bashing the government over corruption, women's safety and, most of all, so-called Muslim appeasement. Once he came to power, Modi had digested that hard political lesson and was determined to ensure that it would not happen to him.

This was relatively easy to do, given the Indian media's structure. Owned by large corporations who looked to court favour with the government, India's powerful national television channels bent over backwards for the new prime minister.

In 2022, the majority of shares in NDTV – India's last news network not seen to be pro-Modi – were bought by Gautam Adani, a billionaire seen not only as Modi's close ally but one whose remarkable rise has been seemingly facilitated by his government. The change of NDTV's ownership was like flipping a switch – the network simply stopped doing any critical reporting, leading to an exodus of its top journalists.

If not directly controlled through a proprietor, the Modi government can also influence media houses through ad spending. The main source of advertising income for legacy media houses in

India is the government, and Modi has withheld ads from media houses seen as being critical of it.

Carrot and stick

What happens if a media house does not bend to Modi? The law provides massive powers to the federal government to regulate – and even ban – television networks. In 2022, it peremptorily shut down Malayalam-language news channel MediaOne, citing "national security" as a reason. While the ban was later reversed by the Supreme Court, the action had a chilling effect on news networks, which simply could not afford to be yanked off air overnight.

Starting in 2020, the Modi government employed even harsher provisions against a small, left-wing website called NewsClick.

First, India's severe money-laundering laws were deployed against it.

Not satisfied, the government then charged it under terror legislation, which allows long prison terms to be imposed even before a court pronounces on the guilt of the accused. NewsClick's founder, Prabir Purkayastha, spent more than seven months in jail before the Supreme Court granted him bail.

Modi has not been shy of using similar tactics against the BBC. In 2023, the government launched income tax raids against the British broadcaster's offices in Delhi after the network aired a documentary critical of Modi's role as chief minister in the 2002 anti-Muslim riots in Gujarat.

All this creates a climate where outright violence against journalists is common. Since Modi took power, 28 journalists have been killed. Reporters Without Borders calls India "one of the world's most dangerous countries for the media".

With the traditional media subdued, Modi is now swivelling his guns towards the internet. Last year, the government published the Broadcasting Services (Regulation) Bill, looking to regulate television and internet broadcasters (such as news streaming services). However, this year a new draft significantly expanded the bill's scope to include internet content creators, apparently driven by the critical role social media had played in the general election where Modi sustained considerable losses.

Copies of this bill were circulated privately by the government but then, just as abruptly, the bill was withdrawn.

Even though the exact status of the bill remains unclear – is this truly a withdrawal or a tactical retreat before the final charge? – the provisions in the 2024 draft version are a good pointer as to the scope of Modi's ambitions when it comes to controlling the internet.

It demanded that content creators subjected themselves to a regulatory regime designed expressly to stifle free expression. It called for them to set up "content evaluation committees", which would need to approve the majority of content before broadcast (certain programmes such as news and current affairs programmes were exempt), appoint a grievance officer, and join a government-approved "self-regulatory organisation" to address grievances and ensure compliance with the relevant codes, which would be drafted by the government. A new government-led Broadcast Advisory Council would sit above these self-regulatory organisations.

The entire edifice is a marvel of Orwellian "red tape-ism", not only bringing content creators under government regulation but making them pay for it themselves. This is significant since adherence to the relevant provisions in the bill would represent a significant – perhaps even crippling – cost for small outfits or individuals.

How successful has Modi been in his desire to curb free expression? While he has achieved a substantial number of his goals, it is a credit to India's democratic traditions that the country's media has not bent in its entirety. While major media houses are unlikely to play their role as watchdog, independent media and individual content creators have stepped in to do the job.

The fierce criticism Modi faced when he released the draft of the broadcasting bill is a fine example of how India's democratic traditions are pushing back against such curbs. It is not insignificant that Modi withdrew the draft and has now gone back to the drawing board on trying to control the internet. ✖

Shoaib Daniyal is the political editor of Scroll.in

53(04):28/29|DOI:10.1177/03064220241306597

RIGHT: Indians are increasingly turning to YouTubers such as Dhruv Rathee when they want news

Editor in exile

IAN WYLIE travels to Germany to meet **KYAW MIN SWE**, who made a daring escape from Myanmar

ABOVE: Kyaw Min Swe was an influential journalist in Myanmar for more than 25 years. He now lives in exile with his family in Berlin

A BLACK SQUARE WAS all it took. Veteran journalist Kyaw Min Swe was arrested by the Myanmar military junta in April 2023 after he blacked out his personal Facebook profile – a sign of despair at the bombing of Pazigyi, a village near his hometown in the Sagaing region, which killed more than 100 people including children.

Around 300 people had gathered for the opening of an office of the National Unity government in exile. Eyewitnesses reported that a fighter jet bombed the village before a helicopter fired on those escaping. It was one of the deadliest attacks on civilians since the military coup in 2021.

Kyaw, the former editor-in-chief of weekly newspaper Aasan (The Voice) and executive director of the Myanmar Journalism Institute, has been a journalist for more than 25 years. He had been detained before, but this time was different.

"On a popular Telegram account that monitors high-profile people like me, I was accused of supporting the People's Defence Force [the PDF is the military wing of the exiled government] and opposing the military with that Facebook post," he told Index. He was summoned to the military interrogation centre in Yangon to explain himself.

"I had nine days of torture – not physical, but mental: three interrogators, working in rotation, asking me the same questions and depriving me of sleep.

"They lied about arresting my reporters, pretending they had evidence of connections with the exiled government and the PDF, but they had nothing. I simply told them the truth: I'm a professional journalist, not pro-exiled government or anti-military, but I disagree with the coup."

Later, he was bundled into a vehicle with a bag over his head.

"I was scared. This was different to my previous experiences," said Kyaw, who was taken first to the police interrogation centre and then to Sanchaung Township police station, where he was charged under Section 505A of Myanmar's Penal Code – used by the junta to target those seen to criticise the regime and carrying a maximum three-year prison sentence.

After almost three months, including two spent in chains in the notorious Insein Prison, he was finally released – with an order to report weekly to police.

"From then on, I was monitored constantly," he said. "The military actually offered me financial support, but they wanted to use me as propaganda and I knew that was professional suicide."

While detained, Kyaw decided he and his family needed to leave Myanmar.

"It was no longer the right place for my kids," he said.

He contacted a friend at Deutsche Welle, the German state broadcaster which part-funds the Myanmar Journalism Institute, and last October he fled Yangon under cover of darkness with his wife and two children.

The daring escape to Germany via Thailand included crossing rivers, trekking through jungles, climbing walls and sheltering in safe houses. Eight months later, with the help of the Exile

Hub, an arm of German non-profit Media in Co-operation and Transition (MiCT), they finally found safety in Berlin in June 2024.

"For my kids it was like an adventure, but not for my wife, who spent seven months taking Xanax because she couldn't sleep," said Kyaw. "She was anxious every time she saw someone in a uniform. In Myanmar, she'd got used to hiding my laptop in the washing machine every time the doorbell rang."

Over the course of his career in Myanmar, Kyaw has seen censorship fluctuate between brief periods of hope and progress to crushing repression.

Before 2011, the military junta imposed strict censorship on the press. Independent media was non-existent, with most newspapers being government-owned or strictly controlled, focusing on state propaganda. Kyaw's media house, for example, was owned by the son of the military intelligence chief.

Journalists had to submit their work to the Press Scrutiny and Registration Division (PSRD) before publication, and any critical or sensitive content – particularly related to the military, politics or ethnic conflicts – was censored. Kyaw said his magazine was suspended six times, sometimes for infringements as minor as running adverts that mentioned neighbouring Thailand.

With the shift to a quasi-civilian government under president Thein Sein in 2011, Myanmar experienced a brief period of media liberalisation. As secretary at Myanmar's Press Council, Kyaw helped draft a media law to protect journalists. The PSRD was abolished, private newspapers were allowed to publish daily, and journalists, for the first time, began to report on previously forbidden subjects.

Yet they still faced threats and prosecution. Kyaw was sued for defamation by the Ministry of Mines in 2012 for publishing a story about alleged misuse of public funds, based on a report from the parliamentary watchdog.

"The ministry demanded a front-page apology, but the parliament report was so clear, we politely declined," he said.

The case dragged on for months and Kyaw faced dozens of court appearances before it was dropped, following pressure from human rights NGOs and a ministerial reshuffle. Kyaw took this as a sign of progress.

Aung San Suu Kyi's National League for Democracy (NLD) came to power in 2016, but the military retained significant power and media freedom deteriorated again.

"We expected a lot from the NLD," recalled Kyaw. "We self-censored and hesitated to criticise them because people loved them so much. We didn't want to be labelled pro-military."

Several high-profile cases of media repression occurred, notably the jailing of Reuters journalists Wa Lone and Kyaw Soe Oo for reporting military atrocities against the Rohingya.

In 2017, Kyaw was arrested in his newsroom along with columnist Ko Kyaw Zwa Naing after a military official complained about a satirical article published in response to a film commemorating Armed Forces Day. Charges against Ko Kyaw Zwa Naing were dropped, but Kyaw Min Swe remained in Insein Prison for two months, on trial for "online defamation" under the 2013 Telecommunications Law.

"They treated us decently because the international community was watching," Kyaw recalled. "The military, and even the Press Council, wanted me to apologise, but I said, 'I'm sorry, this is satire, a form of art. If I apologise, my career is gone'."

The military coup of 2021 dramatically reversed any media freedoms that had been gained. The military seized control of all state media, revoking the licences of independent news outlets such as Mizzima, Myanmar Now and DVB.

"Every journalist was watched and monitored," Kyaw said. "Many journalists were arrested, others were beaten at demonstrations on the street."

Draconian laws were passed, including Section 505(A) of the Penal Code which criminalises "causing fear, spreading false news, or agitating against government employees". Kyaw's newspaper was forced to cease publishing when businesses switched their advertising to state-owned media.

Myanmar has become the world's second biggest jailer of journalists, second only to China, according to Reporters Without Borders (RSF).

Several "exiled media" outlets such as The Irrawaddy have relocated to Thailand and rely on citizen journalists to provide content. Kyaw said he hoped bodies such as the Myanmar Journalism Institute might act as platforms to attract funding for exiled media, as well as for journalists still working inside the country for regional or ethnic media houses. But this can also be problematic.

"Some [exiled] Myanmar media report only what's happening in the war, and only when it's good news for the PDF and the exiled government. But Myanmar people have a right to know true information, free of bias, about the war, the economy or even natural disasters that are happening," Kyaw said. "Without that reporting, our people cannot prepare for the future." ✖

> The ministry demanded a front-page apology, but the parliament report was so clear, we politely declined

Ian Wylie is a freelance journalist who writes for The Guardian and Financial Times and makes documentaries for BBC Radio 4

Evading scrutiny

The covert announcement of Sophia Huang Xueqin and Wang Jianbing's trial verdict shows that China has found a new way to avoid international criticism, writes **BETH CHENG**

ABOVE: Chinese journalist and #MeToo activist Sophia Huang Xueqin, who was arrested in 2021

ON 10 SEPTEMBER 2024, the Higher People's Court of Guangdong Province issued its final verdict in the second trial of feminist journalist Sophia Huang Xueqin and labour activist Wang Jianbing without informing their lawyers. The court rejected their appeals and upheld the original jail sentences – five years for Huang and three and a half years for Wang, under the charge of "inciting subversion of state power".

Despite the lawyers' objection to a written verdict and insistence on a public trial, the Higher Court proceeded. Huang's lawyer Xu Kai accused the court of a "procedural violation" and said it was "depriving the right to defence" because China's Criminal Procedure Law requires all verdicts to be announced publicly – and that verdicts should be delivered to defendants and their lawyers at the same time.

But Xu found out about it only when he met Huang at her detention centre on 13 September. "I was shocked to learn that… the Guangdong High People's Court rejected her appeal and upheld the original verdict," he said in a statement.

Xu expressed his anger at the case's conclusion, as he had spoken to the judge the day before he saw Huang and nothing had been said about the appeal being rejected or the final verdict having already been issued.

A spokesperson for the campaign group Free XueBing (Free Huang Xueqin and Wang Jianbing), who goes by the name of Rio, told Index it was clear that the Higher Court was eager to conclude the case quickly. On one hand, the court's written verdict in the second trial showed the lengths to which the government would go to clamp down on free speech and human rights – even if it meant violating the law. On the other hand, the procedure violation was merely China's new strategy to circumvent the pressure it would face from the international community if the trial had been publicly conducted, due to its unjust handling of the case.

And this strategy worked, to a great extent. Compared with the widespread reporting from international mainstream media on the first hearing and the first verdict, there is scarce news coverage in the West on the handling of the second trial and the final verdict. As for the few reports by Chinese online media outlets, they were, unsurprisingly, scrubbed by the authorities.

"I think it's really a question for the international media," said Rio. "The Chinese government has no intention of stopping their political oppression whatsoever, but its tactics for dealing with international media and aid are continuously evolving… Then the question for the media becomes: 'When the regime keeps abusing the law, and adopts more and more secret operations to reduce attention and supervision from the outside, how should the international media and community deal with this new normal?'"

Contrary to the authorities' apparent aim to conclude the case quickly, it took them nearly two years to begin the first trial after arresting Huang and Wang in December 2021, and another nine months to issue the first verdict in June.

During that time, the authorities were busy gathering evidence to back up their allegations of inciting subversion of state power. This "subversion" included meeting friends and fellow activists to discuss social issues and participating in online social media groups deemed "sensitive" by the government.

According to Rio, merely "liking" group pages on Facebook – a normal exercise of the right to freedom of expression as protected in the constitution

> **When the regime keeps abusing the law, how should the international media and community deal with this new normal?**

– was also considered subversion.

However, in China, neither free speech nor the constitution works, as there is no effective mechanism for initiating an independent constitutional review. "Pocket crimes" – those that are broad and open to interpretation and abuse by law enforcement – are notoriously vague, even unconstitutional, and have been frequently abused. As the prominent Chinese legal scholar Jiang Ping once succinctly remarked, "having a constitution does not equal having constitutionalism".

The fact that Huang and Wang's regular gatherings with friends and discussions of social issues, both online and offline, formed a large part of their "crimes" is telling in terms of China's crackdown on free speech and dissent.

"The political retaliation against XueBing and the regime's fear of them demonstrates the kind of deterrent effect the authorities want to achieve," said Rio. "Since more than 70 others in the community have been targeted and harassed over the years due to this case, it is obvious that the government aims to impose a chilling effect on the civil society community through the XueBing case."

As the famous Chinese saying goes: "Kill the chicken to scare the monkey", which means to make an example out of someone to threaten others. This is the government's goal here, except the chickens are not spooked just yet. Both Huang and Wang have made it clear that they will continue to appeal, despite the verdict. Their next step might be to request the Supreme People's Court to provide opinions and seek a retrial, and Rio said that their lawyers and supporters would continue to back their appeal.

Reacting to her verdict, Huang said: "I was very shocked to receive such a hasty and unjust judgment… This judgment not only disregards the

> Compared with the widespread reporting on the first verdict, there is scarce news coverage in the West on the handling of the second trial

facts but also maliciously speculates, deliberately misinterprets, reverses right and wrong and even contains contradictions. This is a judgment that goes against objective facts and is unjust and inequitable. I don't accept it."

For the Free XueBing campaign group, the secrecy of the final verdict exemplifies once again the unlawful and unfair nature of this case, whilst also demonstrating the government's new strategy of avoiding international media attention and public opinion.

However, Huang and Wang's supporters are determined to continue speaking out, and so should the international community and anyone who cares about free expression. ✖

Sophia Xueqin Huang was a winner in Index's 2022 Freedom of Expression Awards, in the journalism category

Beth Cheng is a freelance journalist who writes about censorship, feminism and culture in China

53(04):32/33|DOI:10.1177/03064220241306617

RIGHT: Police officers stand guard outside a court in Hong Kong in November 2024, where 47 activists and former legislators were charged with conspiring to subvert state power under the National Security Law

ABOVE: Since the Taliban took control of Afghanistan in 2021, homeschooling has been the only option for girls over 11

Lowering the bar

RUTH GREEN speaks to Afghan women who have had their legal careers abruptly halted by the Taliban

AFTER THREE YEARS of Taliban rule, nobody really believed women could be erased further from public life in Afghanistan.

"But the Taliban found another way: they've restricted our voices and faces," said Maryam, an Afghan legal scholar and journalist.

Maryam, who uses a pseudonym, was referring to the Taliban's "vice and virtue" laws, which were passed in August and ban women from speaking, singing or showing their faces in public. If women break the rules, they – or their male relatives – face imprisonment.

Maryam spoke to Index in hushed tones over Signal from the relative safety of her living room in Afghanistan.

The new laws typify the rapid intensification of the Taliban's crackdown, which has already seen women banned from parks, workplaces, schools and universities since it took power in August 2021. Once implemented monthly, harsh laws, decrees, house raids and arrests are now a daily occurrence.

"It's a very intense attack on the dignity of humans and the dignity of women," said Shaharzad Akbar, executive director of Afghan rights group Rawadari. "Before, there was some wiggle room, but it's very scary because now it's law, it's out there and people are required to comply with it."

The crackdown isn't manifesting just through new laws.

"The Taliban have also been destroying institutions and putting new institutions in place to actually implement and carry out their vision of society," said Akbar. She should know, having chaired the Afghan Independent Human Rights Commission before

CREDIT: Ruby / Alamy

it was abruptly dismantled when the Taliban toppled Kabul.

At that time, Maryam was on the cusp of completing her legal training, having graduated from university, and working as an assistant lawyer in the country's courts, often assisting on highly sensitive divorce and domestic violence cases that drew the ire of Taliban members.

After the takeover, the Taliban closed the country's only bar association. All existing licences to practise law were revoked, putting lawyers out of work. Many like Maryam, who were still waiting for their licences to be formally approved, never received their documentation. As the Taliban filled the Ministry of Justice and the courts with its own lawyers, judges and prosecutors, Maryam's chances of a legal career vanished.

Maryam was just a toddler when the Taliban was overthrown in 2001. Now 26 years old, she finds it hard speaking about the early "bad days" after the Taliban's recent return to power and the subsequent unravelling of decades of progress on women's rights.

She has relatives – mostly judges and their immediate families – who have managed to leave the country. Yet, like many Afghans, she's not been deemed enough "at risk" to warrant evacuation. Instead, she's focused on doing what she can while living under the constant threat of Taliban restrictions.

Through word of mouth, she established a homeschool teaching English to girls in her neighbourhood. It was one of the many underground schools that proliferated across Afghanistan after September 2021 when the Taliban issued a ban on girls over the age of 11 attending secondary school.

However, as rumours swirled about the rising number of secret schools, the authorities began doing door-to-door searches. She received messages over Telegram from Taliban fighters warning that she'd be thrown into jail if she didn't stop "working against the regime".

Maryam said she had no choice but to close the school.

"We already were in danger because of the position of my family in the justice system," she said. "I didn't want to make more danger for myself, my family or my students."

In December 2022, the Taliban banned all Afghan women from attending university. Maryam's husband, an engineer, was teaching at a local university, and he was devastated that his female students were being forced to give up their studies.

Under the most recent law, he faces losing his job if he leaves work to accompany Maryam anywhere. Without him, she's forbidden from leaving the house.

The Taliban has created hundreds of positions for men to teach in gender-segregated religious schools – *madrassas* – across the country, while women with university degrees and teaching experience are forced to stay at home.

Rawadari – one of the few organisations that has maintained a network on the ground documenting violations of civil and political rights since the takeover – has been closely following the detrimental impact of the education ban on women's and girls' mental health across Afghanistan's 34 provinces.

The overwhelming sense of 'hopelessness' is undeniable, said Akbar, who now lives in the UK in exile but still finds reports of what's happening back home extremely difficult to hear.

"I think most of the girls believed this will be temporary and never imagined they would experience what their mothers had experienced," she said. "They are depressed and they're struggling to keep their hopes alive."

Maryam continues to battle her own mental health struggles as a result of the restrictions, but has found some solace in working in the shadows as an online educator, mental health trainer, journalist and advocate.

However, as the internet and social media platforms are increasingly monitored by the Taliban and its spies, she has had to be more careful about her online interactions.

"I can't trust who is safe and who is not," she said. "There are women on Instagram and other places who are looking for women who are disobeying Taliban rule. For that reason, I don't share anything about myself. They just hear my voice and the teachings I'm offering them. I'm scared and my colleagues are scared, but we go forward, do the job and provide teaching for those who need it."

Unsilenced in exile

There is also growing momentum from Afghan women internationally to give their sisters inside the country a voice. One such woman is Qazi Marzia Babakarkhail, who became a judge in Afghanistan at 26 – the same age that Maryam is now.

Babakarkhail worked in the family courts, later setting up a small shelter for divorced women in Afghanistan and a school for Afghan refugees in Pakistan. Those initiatives were a lifeline to dozens of women, but they soon drew unwanted attention from the Taliban and she fled the country in 2008 after two assassination attempts.

Since moving to the UK, Babakarkhail has learnt English and now works as a caseworker for an MP

> She received messages over Telegram from Taliban fighters warning that she'd be thrown into jail if she didn't stop "working against the regime"

New developments are already reviving dreams that Afghan women's rights and freedoms will one day be restored

→ near Manchester. As well as helping campaign for the evacuation of hundreds of female judges, she speaks daily to former colleagues and friends still trapped in Afghanistan.

Her advocacy earned her an invitation to an all-Afghan women's summit held in Tirana, Albania, in September. It was the first time since the Taliban regained power that such a large group of Afghan women – more than 100 from across Europe, the USA, Canada and Afghanistan itself – had been given an international platform to discuss the rollback of women's rights. They are so often excluded from conversations on Afghanistan's future.

This marked a sharp contrast with a UN meeting held earlier in June in Doha, which was heavily criticised for inviting Taliban leaders and neglecting to bring Afghan women's voices to the table.

Babakarkhail said the summit had opened 'a new window of hope' for Afghan women. Seeing women who defied the Taliban travel to Tirana reminded her of her own perilous journey and gave her hope for Afghanistan's future.

"They are real activists because they are still fighting and still stay in Afghanistan," she said. "Of course they do a lot of things silently, but they will go back. They know how to deal with the Taliban and they will keep silent. They made us proud."

She is hopeful the summit – which discussed the unravelling human rights situation, the urgent need for humanitarian aid and international recognition of the Taliban's mistreatment of women as "gender apartheid" – will provide the necessary wake-up call to the international community.

"We don't want the United Nations or other countries to recognise the Taliban as a government," she said. "This group is a stand against the Taliban and a stand for people in Afghanistan."

Pushing for accountability

The international push for accountability, both at the International Criminal Court – which has an ongoing investigation into alleged crimes committed in Afghanistan – and the groundbreaking move to bring a gender persecution case against the Taliban at the International Court of Justice (ICJ) – are other signs that the dial may finally be shifting in Afghan women's favour.

Akbar has been one of the leading voices campaigning to bring the case to the ICJ. Although she is appalled by what is happening to her motherland, she believes these judicial measures and the summit in Tirana will help ensure Afghan women's voices are no longer silenced.

"We have a saying in Farsi," said Akbar. "We say, 'Drop by drop, you make a river.' All of this will come together to become this river of hope and this river of defiance against the Taliban. The dream really is that we show the Taliban that the power of people everywhere in the world is with the women of Afghanistan and not with them."

For Maryam, such developments are already reviving dreams that Afghan women's rights and freedoms will one day be restored.

"I know that the suffering that women are enduring under the Taliban's gender apartheid regime is unique," she said.

She hopes the ongoing efforts, both by women like her inside the country and by those elsewhere in the world, will be enough.

"We are motivating and inspiring each other. We will win and the future will be ours – women's." ✖

Ruth Green is a journalist who writes about law, business and human rights

53(04):34/36|DOI:10.1177/03064220241306618

RIGHT: Despite Lady Justice being a symbol of morality and impartiality worldwide, women can no longer practise law in Afghanistan

CREDIT: Stefanski / Alamy

A promise is a promise

Argentina's president vowed to attack the press – and he has delivered. **AMY BOOTH** reports

PUNK MUSIC BLARED through the speakers. The crowd roiled like a moshpit. Argentina's president Javier Milei – clad in a leather jacket – strutted onto the stage, hugged his sister and roared along to the lyrics.

Then the attacks began.

The president was at a rally to launch La Libertad Avanza (Freedom Advances), his minority ruling coalition, as a political party.

"The journalistic caste, those corrupt microphones, did a media blackout of us that day," Milei said, referring to an early rally during his political ascent.

"That same day, the media's reality began to change. Listen to me, journalists who take bribes, this is how people feel about you."

His supporters booed and jeered.

Throughout his speech, he described journalists as "pieces of shit" and "hitman professionals", claimed his followers had "shut them the hell up", and made baseless allegations of corruption. It was a disturbing tirade, and one that journalists have heard with alarming frequency over the past year.

Milei was elected president in November 2023. An eccentric far-right economist who preached hardcore libertarianism, he railed against political elites he called the "caste" and promised to take a chainsaw to state spending – a point he liked to underscore by waving an actual chainsaw around at rallies.

But one year into his government,

ABOVE: President Javier Milei speaks to supporters during a rally in Buenos Aires in 2023

Milei has made it abundantly clear that the ideals of freedom he so ardently preaches do not extend to journalists and other critical voices. Since taking office, he has shut down the newswire of Argentina's public news agency, clamped down on freedom of information requests and has made a habit of personally attacking journalists through social media.

Dozens of journalists have been injured in a crackdown on protests, and reporters, social media users and other critical voices have been mobbed by groups of trolls who have a murky relationship with the government. It has resulted in Argentina falling 26 places in the Reporters Without Borders 2024 World Press Freedom Index.

On Monday 4 March, reporters at public news agency Télam showed up to work to find that their offices had been fenced off and police were outside, refusing to let them in. The website, a wire service of news, videos and photos from all over the country, had been shut down.

At 9pm the previous Friday, Milei had attacked the agency in a speech to open congress after the summer recess, calling it an opposition "propaganda agency" and promising to shut it down.

At the time, Télam employed around 700 journalists. Its services were used by media of all stripes in Argentina, and it played a particularly important role in providing information from across the country's 24 provinces. The workers were sent on paid leave.

It wasn't clear how the government could close Télam. Legally, it was required to go via congress, which it had not done – yet it seemed bent on closing the agency anyway.

What followed was a four-month standoff. Télam journalists set up a protest camp outside their former

In 10 months of government, over 100 journalists were attacked with rubber bullets

offices, although around 400 took voluntary redundancy.

Finally, in July, it was announced that some of Télam's staff would be incorporated into Argentina's other public media. Télam itself was turned into an agency called APESAU, dedicated to state advertising and publicity – functions it had also fulfilled previously.

Personal attacks

The president is an obsessive user of social media, especially X.

In early October, he spent up to five hours a day on the site, sharing as many as 482 posts daily, according to estimates from milei.nulo.in, a bot dedicated to tracking how much time the president spends tweeting.

Sometimes he posts screeds against the press. In a long post in August, he claimed that many journalists disliked social media because they had lost "monopoly of the microphone" and could be fact-checked more easily.

"They're crying because they've lost the power to lie, slander, insult and even extort [people] at no cost," he wrote. "Obviously, and without a doubt, the dirtier the journalist and the darker their past, the more they hate social media."

In the post, he tagged X owner and business magnate Elon Musk, who he said had rid the platform of "woke censorship". The pair have met three times, and Musk has expressed interest in investing in Argentina since Milei took office.

But the president doesn't stop at insulting the press as a whole. He has frequently used his platform to attack individual journalists whom he perceives as the enemy.

"Evidently, we're living in a very hostile climate for our work," radio journalist María O'Donnell told the congressional commission on freedom of expression in September. "Especially due to what's happening on social media, with the president himself getting involved in certain attacks, which he tends to justify by claiming that he has the right to express himself to refute journalists' lies."

O'Donnell has been targeted by Milei, who has taken her clips out of context to accuse her of lying and posted criticisms of her for attending the Copa América football tournament.

"There is an attempt to discredit the person, not the work – what North Americans call 'character assassination'," she said.

Jorge Fontevecchia, president and chief executive officer of the newspaper Perfil, sued Milei after the president called him, among other things, an "enveloped journalist" – a reference to journalists' supposed corruption. On 10 October, Judge Sebastián Ramos ruled that no offence had been committed. Fontevecchia plans to appeal. A similar lawsuit by journalist Jorge Lanata remains open.

"[Milei] seeks to take away substance, legitimacy and trust in journalism," said Alicia Miller, of the Argentine Journalism Forum, which monitors press freedom. "The president, before he was president, trusted in a direct connection between him and his followers through social media, so he believes journalism has become irrelevant. But journalism is an irreplaceable tool for the flow of information in a free society."

In some cases, these attacks on press freedom veer into the bizarre. Milei famously had a pet English mastiff named Conan, who was his closest companion in the years before he shot to fame as a vociferous television pundit.

When Conan died, he hired a US company named PerPETuate to clone him. Five puppies were shipped out to Argentina in 2018.

After that, the details are sketchy: Milei is understood to have five dogs, four of which are named after his favourite economists. However, in photos, he only appears with four of them. Any journalists seeking a definitive answer from the government will find themselves frustrated, however. Treasury prosecutor Rodolfo Barra ruled in July that they were off limits to public inquiry because they were part of Milei's private life.

Then, in September, the government introduced a series of changes to what things were subject to freedom of information requests. It meant Conan questions were out for good but it also had the more serious consequence of excluding documents such as those relating to private companies working with the state, and the paperwork that goes into the formulation of laws.

Digital violence

On social media, Milei's critics are often hit by a tsunami of insults, abuse and threats from pro-government trolls. Some X users have suffered doxxing (the publication of their personal information) and other strategies that take the violence offline.

An investigation by Crisis magazine found that users had received death threats, found threatening banners hung outside their homes and had strangers turning up on their doorsteps after fraudulent Facebook Marketplace adverts were published with their addresses.

In the more extreme cases, government involvement has not been demonstrated. However, Juan Pablo Carreira, a troll known as Juan Doe, was appointed as the director of digital communications for the president's office, while entry records for Casa Rosada – the president's executive mansion and office – showed that another notorious troll, known as El Gordo Dan (Fat Dan), was a frequent visitor.

Violence and harassment against journalists isn't limited to the digital realm. There has been a dramatic increase in the number of press workers injured by police while covering protests.

Journalism has to annoy. That's its mission

ABOVE: An anti-government protester wearing a dog mask holds up a sign that reads "You cloned poverty", a reference to President Javier Milei's cloning of his deceased English mastiff Conan

In December, Milei announced a long presidential decree and an even longer congressional bill that, between them, deregulated vast swathes of Argentina's economy. They stripped workers' rights, attacked environmental protections and granted Milei emergency powers.

When the bill was sent for debate in congress, social movements, unions, neighbourhood associations and other groups flocked to the square outside the legislature to protest. They were met with a fierce police crackdown. Officers used rubber bullets, a water cannon and tear gas against the crowd and dozens of people were arrested.

More than 30 journalists in the square covering the protest were injured. Some were shot with rubber bullets at close range despite being identified as members of the press. The nature of the violence prompted unions and rights organisations to ask the Inter-American Commission on Human Rights for protective measures. This marked a dramatic escalation in police repression of journalists, according to Agustín Lecchi, secretary general of journalists' union Sipreba.

"In 10 months of government, over 100 journalists were attacked with rubber bullets [and] tear gas," he told Index. "That didn't happen before."

Lecchi argued that this was part of a government strategy to silence criticism of controversial policies on issues such as mining and oil and gas extraction, and to hide the human impact of police brutality.

"They don't want [journalists] to show pictures of repressive forces repressing pensioners," he said. "It's not a coincidence that they're going for photographers."

Many critics have noted the apparent contradiction of a president who preaches the "ideas of liberty" on stage before clamping down on freedom of expression from the presidential office.

"Governments are always annoyed by journalism," said Miller. "[Journalism] has to annoy. That's its mission, its nature … Nourishing journalism, tolerating criticism – that's not an option, it's a constitutional obligation." ✖

Amy Booth is a journalist covering South America

ABOVE: The Russian news outlet Meduza ultimately had to go into exile and is now headquartered in Riga, Latvia

Going offline

STEVE KOMARNYCKYJ explores how internet censorship laws and cultural bans are creating a new Iron Curtain in Russia and Belarus

METALLICA HAVE BEEN blacklisted in Russia. The band were among 79 artists, including Beyoncé and Lana Del Ray, on a list circulated among Russian advertising agencies and event organisers, with recipients urged not to use the artists' songs in advertising campaigns or at public events, according to The Moscow Times.

The ban reflects the Kremlin's clampdown over recent years on information it does not control and on websites that could enable the organisation of protests or gatherings.

In October, Apple removed Current Time – a TV and digital network run by Free Europe/Radio Liberty – from its app store in Russia, at the request of the country's media regulatory agency. Discord, a gaming platform which has been used to organise protests and discuss politics, was also blocked in October after it was found to be "violating Russian law" by hosting content such as criticism of the invasion of Ukraine.

In 2019, a "sovereign internet" law was passed, essentially severing Russia's internet from the worldwide web, opening the door to greater online censorship. Measures announced this year give the state even more powers to block access to the internet, with more than half a billion dollars allocated to improve a digital system that censors web traffic.

I contacted human rights organisations the Centre for Civil Liberties in Ukraine, and Russia's International Memorial to discuss this clampdown on free speech.

I also contacted the Viasna Human Rights Centre, based in Belarus, which was not able to comment. Its founder, Ales Bialiatski, was jailed for 10 years in March 2023 on fabricated charges. He had been a recipient of the Nobel Peace Prize, alongside International Memorial and the Centre for Civil Liberties.

International Memorial would only comment under an anonymous representative – many of its activists have been arrested and co-chair Oleg Orlov was charged last year with discrediting the Russian armed forces after he criticised the war in Ukraine.

The Centre for Civil Liberties is the only group of the three able to challenge its government free of harassment.

I asked Oleksandra Romantsova, its executive director, if the online situation in Ukraine really was preferable to that in Russia or Belarus. She noted there was "absolute pluralism" on the Ukrainian internet but observed that the president's office had occasionally instructed state TV channels how to cover news. United News, a TV programme initially set up to give Ukrainians access to important information when the Russian invasion began in 2022, had been criticised for becoming a state tool to control content.

She also acknowledged that, despite the freedom of the Ukrainian internet, Ukrainska Pravda, the country's most popular online news site, recently put out a statement saying it had been pressured by the president's office. Historically, the organisation has been a staunch defender of free speech – its co-founder, Georgiy Gongadze, had been a fierce and fearless critic of the government, and was ultimately abducted and murdered in September 2000 near Kyiv. A recording later emerged of then president Leonid Kuchma implying that the journalist's death was desirable.

However, Romantsova said that the situation was different from in Russia, where internet servers collect data on users to be handed over to intelligence services and police as required. This has dovetailed with a law against "discrediting" the Russian army, adopted as part of a package of war censorship laws in 2022. She said that there were regional targets for arresting people under these laws – a key reason that many media outlets, such as Meduza and TV Rain, have gone into exile.

The laws have impacted my ability to speak to people for this article. A spokesperson from International Memorial argued that Russia's internet laws "created an unprecedented system of restricting civil liberties".

In particular there are three

Belarus, like Russia, is increasingly sealed off from the global internet, banning musicians and targeting journalists

dangerous principles in the legislation, they said. These are the "vague wording of the laws", the "extrajudicial procedure for blocking [sites]", and the lack of an appeals process. These combine to allow the state "maximum powers with minimum responsibility". While Russia remains linked to the web, the blocking of sites has increased exponentially, major platforms such as YouTube essentially do not work, and VPNs are blocked for refusing to filter content. According to Reporters Without Borders, more than 1.7 million URLs, including those of media outlets, are now blocked in Russia.

It is not only the legal framework that is stifling freedom of expression but also the unsolved murders of reporters. When investigative journalist Anna Politkovskaya was murdered on 7 October 2006, president Vladimir Putin's birthday, he vowed to bring her killers to justice. However, no one was ever prosecuted for commissioning her killing and mysterious deaths of journalists continue.

Belarus, like Russia, is increasingly sealed off from the global internet, banning musicians and targeting journalists. Cher and Lady Gaga were reportedly banned from performing in the country in February 2023. I contacted Hanna Liubakova, a Belarusian journalist living in exile, about freedom of speech in her home country. She said "independent journalists face ... constant threats, with the regime targeting their families".

She added: "At least 36 media professionals are currently imprisoned, including my friends ... Ihar Losik and Katsiaryna Andreeva. Few journalists can safely report from inside the country, making critical coverage of the regime nearly impossible."

However, she emphasised that there was a "resilient network ... with thousands of Belarusians contributing information to projects like Belarusian Hajun [an activism project monitoring military activity of Russian and Belarusian troops in Belarus], while others are documenting the situation. These efforts, alongside the bravery of exiled journalists, are essential in preserving any semblance of truth". Liubakova herself has been sentenced in absentia to 10 years in prison on baseless charges of "seizing power" and "extremism".

The increasing severance of the internet in Belarus and Russia is sealing these countries into an informational and cultural bubble, increasing regression rather than progression. In the words of Metallica's Enter Sandman, which fewer Russians can now listen to, "Exit light, enter night". ✖

Steve Komarnyckyj is a British-Ukrainian writer and linguist

53(04):40/41|DOI:10.1177/03064220241306973

ABOVE: Czech Foreign Minister Jan Lipavsky at the awarding of the Nobel Peace Prize to human rights organisation International Memorial in Oslo in 2022

ABOVE AND RIGHT: Readers gather at the Hazrat Shah Waliullah Public Library in 2018

The beacon of hope

Author and filmmaker **NILOSREE BISWAS** reflects on the tranquility of Hazrat Shah Waliullah Public Library, situated in a divided Delhi

OLD DELHI – or Purani Dilli (its local name) – is chaotic, with its congested lanes, honking rickshaws, crumbling buildings housing generations of families, rows of shops which sell almost everything under the sun and the whiff of spices and oil in the air from delectable Mughal dishes served by century-old eateries.

For the unversed, Old Delhi was formerly known as the Mughal city Shahjahanabad, one of the oldest populated areas of India's capital, New Delhi.

At the heart of this bustling neighbourhood is a non-descript public library, all in one room, which quietly nurtures the power of syncretic knowledge and collective learning. Hazrat Shah Waliullah Public Library, simply called "library" by the locals, was born in 1987. Now, 37 years later, it is perhaps one of the most meditative public spaces in Delhi, although its genesis was rooted in tense circumstances.

Hindu-Muslim communal clashes and riots ravaged Old Delhi in May 1987. Curfews were imposed for days, resulting in a shortage of supplies – milk in particular. The situation was discomfiting for local shop owners Mohammad Naeem and Sikander Mirza Changezi (later the founding members of the library), and others.

They decided to volunteer to deliver provisions, spending the rest of their time playing the table game carrom in a tiny room of a dilapidated house. The act of delivering provisions impacted them and kindled a sense of purpose in them.

Naeem's quiet demeanour visibly perks up as he recalls the birth of the library. "We discussed what may work best for the community in the long term and came up with the decision to work in school education," he said.

"Our primary aim was to prevent the large number of dropouts from the neighbourhood. To roll out our tiny initiative, we formed a grassroots community organisation and registered ourselves as a not-for-profit, naming it Delhi Youth Welfare Association, and in 1990 established Hazrat Shah Waliullah Public Library. Hardly did we know what the future had in store for us!"

Nearly 40 years later, as libraries and *madrassas* (Islamic schools) are being set on fire by frenzied far-right Hindutva mobs, the humble library has held its ground. With one of India's largest collections of books in Urdu – along with Arabic, Hindi and English titles – this one room is a hive of knowledge, housing more than 30,000 books.

Among them is a priceless reserve of rare books – a holy Quran that is more than a century old, written in multiple calligraphic styles with gold embossing; the original volume of poetry by the last Mughal emperor, Bahadur Shah Zafar, titled Diwan-e-Zafar and published in 1885, with the year marked with the official emblem of the royal press; a

130-year-old multilingual dictionary by Sultan Shah Jahan Begum, the ruler of the princely state of Bhopal; the cult 19th-century poet Mirza Ghalib's ever popular work, Diwan-e-Ghalib; a holy Bhagavat Gita, written in Urdu and published by one of the earliest publishers and printers in India, The Nawal Kishore Press; and rare treatises of Sufi teachings.

Naeem reflects on how the robust collection came about.

"Having named the library after [the] revered 18th-century Naqshbandi Islamic Sufi scholar and reformer Shah Waliullah, we donated our personal collection first. Then public donations started coming in. Sometimes complete strangers would approach us with the intent of donating. Today these donations make [up] 60% [of our] books, and the rest we have purchased. [In] those days we explored the book bazaar of Daryaganj every Sunday and found surprising treasures like the Bhagavat Gita in Urdu.

"Scholars started dropping by, some of them [from] faculties in universities in the USA and the UK. Since we also own Shah Waliullah's complete original works, those researching him make sure to visit us."

The library has transformed into a seeker's paradise, from researchers in higher studies to high-school students on the lookout for textbooks.

"We initiated the culture of upcycling textbooks [and] convinced senior school students to donate their books for the next batch," said Abu Sufiyan, a community leader working with youth groups. "What began with… 22 students, now has a pool of 600." Having so many book donations has helped to prevent students from dropping out of senior school education.

But the library is at a crossroads. With no grants from government or private funding bodies, its future seems bleak. To make matters more complicated there is also a space issue – the collection is already full to the brim, but new donations continue to pour in.

Naeem said they had the opportunity to buy a new plot for a second library four years ago in Mewat, Haryana, but they have yet to pay for it all due to financial constraints.

"We are paying them in slow instalments every time we gather some donations," he said. "I would say the plot owners were kind to still allow construction."

However, the biggest challenge lies in the sustainability of the institution. In the present political climate of India, where Muslim history is becoming increasingly invisible, the chances are that such an initiative would be dismissed as a "Muslim-dominated" project.

But does this mean the library should approach both government and non-governmental donor organisations for support? The answer is both "yes" and "no" – but it would not be simple.

"It's a small team. We have lots on our plate," said Sufiyan. "To follow up on government grants or schemes isn't easy for us. It may involve bureaucracy and can be even more time consuming. As for the private donor organisations, they come with their own agenda. It's a strange situation."

The evening has passed by in a blink – it's now 10.30pm. The reading room is at its best now that it's quiet. But, interestingly, neither the readers nor the members seem to be in a rush to call it a night.

"If we truly wish to serve the community, we must understand their needs," said Sufiyan. "The researchers and scholars have requested us to keep the library open till late as that would be of help. They usually drop in after university hours or their day jobs, so [we] are open till 11 at night."

Outside, the chaos of Old Delhi prevails as I try to navigate the lanes and honking rickshaws. But the million-dollar question is not lost – will this beacon of hope survive? Or will it succumb to these divisive times? ✖

Nilosree Biswas is an author, filmmaker and columnist who writes about the history, culture, food and cinema of South Asia, the Middle East and the Asian diaspora

> There is a space issue for the library – the collection is already full to the brim, but new donations continue to pour in

A story of forgotten fiction

Vietnam's rich literary history has been plagued by censorship, writes **THIỆN VIỆT**

HOÀNG MINH TƯỜNG has published 17 novels. Seven of these have been banned from re-publication or circulation in Vietnam and two had to be published overseas due to political sensitivities. But the Hanoi-based writer remains upbeat.

"I have been blessed by the heavenly gods," said the 76-year-old, who used to work as a teacher and journalist. "Many times, I was afraid that I might be imprisoned. Yet I still remain alive."

The award-winning novelist is currently seeking help to have his best-known novel *Thời của Thánh Thần* (The Time of the Gods) translated into English. On release in 2008, it was widely regarded as a literary phenomenon yet was immediately recalled and has been banned ever since.

Hoàng, and many other writers I spoke to for this article, agreed that censorship is accepted as part of living and working in Vietnam, where the Communist Party monopolises the publishing industry. The 2012 Publishing Law emphasises the need to "fight against all thoughts and behaviour detrimental to the national interests and contribute to the construction and defence of the Socialist Republic of Vietnam".

But censorship of fiction is just one part of the country's free expression quandary. Reporters Without Borders has long categorised Vietnam as being among the worst countries for freedom of the press. The Ministry of Information and Communications (MIC) is the government agency responsible for state management of press, publishing and printing activities. Writers have to regularly negotiate with censors – and then creatively rise above them or patiently wait for the individuals or agencies in charge to change their minds.

Living with censorship

Hoàng, a Communist Party member, said that The Time of the Gods, written between 2005 and 2008, was a turning point in his literary career, which has spanned three decades.

"After finishing writing the book in 2008, my biggest concern was how to get it published," he said. "I gave it to three influential friends in three publishing houses, all of whom rejected it because if they published it they would be sent to jail."

In his banned novel, the characters are multi-faceted. Four brothers navigate different sides of armed conflicts, align with various factions and transcend the simplistic "us versus the enemy" narrative often depicted by the Communist Party.

They endure many of the hidden, historical tribulations of Vietnam – from the Maoist land reform in the 1950s, which seized agricultural land and property owned by landlords for redistribution, to the fall of Saigon in 1975, which ended the Vietnam War and resulted in a mass exodus to escape the victorious communist regime.

"The story of a family is not just the story of a single family but the story of the times, the story of the nation, the story of the two communist and capitalist factions, of the North and South regions of Vietnam and the United States," said Hoàng. "Perhaps that is why, for the past 15 years, tens of thousands of illegal copies of the book have been printed and people still seek it out to read."

The ban has created fertile ground for black market circulation, he said, with online and offline pirated copies often full of mistakes.

There have never been any official government documents justifying the book ban, nor has there been any explanation for the sensitivities surrounding his works.

He asserted that this lack of transparency and accountability was a common occurrence for novelists. "Most of the bans [on my books] were purely by word of mouth," he said.

For years, Hoàng has communicated with editors at the state-owned Writers' Association Publishing House (which originally published the book), but to no avail. However, the novel has made its way to global audiences, being translated into Korean, French, Japanese and Mandarin Chinese.

His 2014 novel *Nguyên khí* (Vitality) was originally rejected for publication, and again reasons were not disclosed. The

ABOVE: A bookstore in Crescent Mall, Ho Chi Minh City, Vietnam, 2023

> The literary landscape in Vietnam is "as limited as political speech itself"

ABOVE: Vietnam's Communist Party general secretary To Lam inspects an honour guard on a visit to Malaysia in November 2024

story, revolving around Nguyễn Trãi – a 15th century historical figure who was a loyal and skilled official falsely accused of killing an emperor – symbolises the still strained relationship between single-party rule and patriotic intellectuals.

In response, Hoàng revised the narrative of the novel by getting rid of a character – a security agent doubling as a censor and eavesdropper. He retitled the work to The Tragedy of a Great Character, a rebranding that managed to pass through pre-print censorship. Subsequently, in 2019, the book was published and sold out. However, its previous ban was soon recognised, so it didn't secure a permit for republication.

Learning from history

In his 2022 article Banishing the Poets: Reflections on Free Speech and Literary Censorship in Vietnam, Richard Quang Anh Trần, assistant professor of Southeast Asian studies at Ca' Foscari University of Venice, concluded that the literary landscape in Vietnam was "as limited as political speech itself".

"The boundaries of permissible speech, moreover, are ever changing that one may find oneself caught in the crosshairs and on the wrong side at any given moment," he wrote.

Trần identified two turning points when writers were fooled into believing that the Communist Party had allowed them to challenge the established literary norms of serving the party.

The first occurred in the 1950s, during a cultural-political movement in Hanoi, called the Nhân Văn-Giai Phẩm Affair. A group of party-loyal writers and intellectuals launched two journals, Nhân Văn (Humanity) and Giai Phẩm (Masterpieces). They sought to convince the party of the need for greater artistic and intellectual freedom. Despite their distinguished service to the state, they were condemned in state media and their publications were banned.

The second case came in the late 1980s and early 1990s during Doi Moi (the Renovation Period), a series of economic and political reforms which started in 1986. Vietnam's market liberalisation breathed new life into war-centric literature, and many writers crafted brilliant post-war novels that challenged prevailing narratives – but their works were censored. This was done through limiting the number of approved copies, recalling and confiscating books →

RIGHT: A pedestrian looks at books in Hanoi, Vietnam

→ from libraries and bookshops, and destroying original drafts.

Censorship was at its worst when the party decided to burn the books of those it regarded as its enemies. Following the fall of Saigon on 30 April 1975, it embarked on a campaign to eliminate what it classified as decadent and reactionary culture, including many books and magazines published in the Republic of Vietnam (South Vietnam).

"South Vietnamese publications were the main target, plus much of popular music, movies and the fine arts," said Dr Tuấn Hoàng, associate professor of great books at Pepperdine University's Seaver College in California. "Government workers entered businesses and private residences suspected of having such materials and took away what they could find."

"Those materials were burned or recycled at factories," he said. "Citizens were urged to give up banned materials to the government, or to destroy them themselves. A lot of materials were therefore destroyed in the first few years after the war."

But some materials were hidden, circulated clandestinely or sold on the black market. Phạm Thị Hoài is one of the most celebrated writers of the post-Renovation Period, whose debut novel The Crystal Messenger was a success both at home and abroad. The first edition (1988) and second edition (1995) were published by the Writers' Association Publishing House, bar a few censored paragraphs, according to Phạm. But it was later banned by the government.

After leaving Vietnam for Germany, in 2001 she established Talawas, an online forum dedicated to reviving literary works by Vietnamese writers. She says she has been banned from travelling back to her home country since 2004, a fact she attributes to Talawas and her literary works, which have been ambiguously deemed to be "sensitive". Her books have not been permitted to be republished in Vietnam.

"A few years ago, a friend in the publishing industry also tried to inquire about reprinting a collection of my short stories, which were entirely about love, but no publishing house accepted it," she said.

In 2018, the government introduced a new cybersecurity law, which has made censorship worse. Critical voices that challenge the state's version of history online are deemed to be hostile forces that are seeking to discredit the party's revolutionary achievements.

Appreciate, don't criticise

Censorship also makes its way into education as, in Vietnam, literature is first and foremost intended to inculcate party-defined patriotism into young minds.

According to Dr Ngọc, a high-school literature teacher in Hanoi, Vietnamese authors who are featured in school textbooks normally have very "red" (communist) backgrounds or hold party leadership positions. She added that the higher an author's position in government, the more focus is given to their work in textbooks. "Many great writers were unfortunately not selected for the literature textbooks," she said.

Ngọc provides tutoring for high-school students to help them prepare for their national entrance exams. These exams mostly focus on wartime hardship and heroism.

Students' responses need to show that they revere communist leaders and revile invaders. But this teaching method is not best placed to help them appreciate literature.

But ill-fated books still find their way to readers, often through the black market. Phương (not her real name) has been selling books in Hanoi for the past two decades. She says that every now and then people still look for banned books, which she collects and sells. However, these are reserved only for her closest customers.

"I would not sell sensitive books to a random buyer," she said. "They might be disguised security agents trying to recall the book from the market." ✖

> Many times, I was afraid that I might be imprisoned. Yet I still remain alive

Thiện Việt is a journalist from Vietnam

SPECIAL REPORT

UNSUNG HEROES: HOW MUSICIANS ARE RAISING THEIR VOICES AGAINST OPPRESSION

"Beyond physical violence, Bobi Wine has also suffered as an artist through the government's ceaseless quest to silence him"

SINGING FOR A REVOLUTION | DANSON KAHYANA | P.74

LEFT: The Afghanistan National Institute of Music is now based in Portugal. Here, they perform at Carnegie Hall in New York in 2024

SPECIAL REPORT ♦ UNSUNG HEROES

The sound of silence

The Taliban's culture ban has put Afghanistan's musicians under serious threat. **SARAH DAWOOD** explores the impact on those in exile and those who remain

WHEN THE TALIBAN seized power in Kabul in August 2021, they soon began searching people's homes for items they deemed to be immoral. Waheedullah Saghar, the head of the music department at Kabul University, had to destroy all of his musical instruments before they were found. Among his collection were special items he'd bought during his time in India, such as a *tanpura* – a traditional folk stringed instrument.

"It was too risky to keep instruments at home," he told Index. "Many of my colleagues also felt forced to destroy their instruments, and we disposed of the broken pieces in the garbage to protect ourselves."

He was denied access to his university and received an official notice from the Taliban that all musical activities in Afghanistan would be prohibited in future.

"It's very strange, because one day we were honourable, respectable people of our city," he said. "Then just one day later we became victims and as if we should be punished, because we were musicians. It was very painful and very difficult."

Saghar and his colleagues were granted asylum in Germany in 2021, and he is currently based in New York on a year-long placement, where he is keeping the culture of his home country alive by teaching university students about Afghan and Indian classical music.

"We had to find a solution for our situation," he said. "Staying in Afghanistan in that critical moment was not an option because our lives were in danger."

His story is similar to those of many musicians who have been either forced to leave or forced to abandon their livelihoods. Musicians in the country live in fear of discrimination, humiliation, torture, imprisonment, sexual violence in the case of women and even death. According to the Associated Press, the family of folk singer Fawad Andarabi accused the Taliban of executing him near his home in a mountain province north of Kabul in 2021.

Since their return in 2021, the Taliban have waged a war on music, claiming that it causes "moral corruption". This approach mirrors their reign between 1996 and 2001, when music was also strictly prohibited. According to figures from its own Ministry for the Propagation of Virtue and the Prevention of Vice, the group has destroyed more than 21,000 musical instruments over the past year, including traditional items such as *tabla* drums and *rubabs*, a type of lute which is Afghanistan's national instrument.

After their takeover of Kabul, the country's public radio station, Radio Afghanistan, was swiftly rebranded Voice of Sharia, and music was removed from radio and TV stations, replaced with religious chanting.

The Taliban's use of chanting shows that there is hypocrisy in their extremism, Saghar says. They are sung without instruments, to inspire patriotism and instil their ideology.

"The Taliban don't seem to understand what music truly represents

SPECIAL REPORT: UNSUNG HEROES

or its role in society," he said. "They claim that music is *haram* ("forbidden") in Islam, without considering its broader meaning and significance. Music is an inseparable part of human life and is even integrated into aspects of Islamic practice.

"For example, the Quran is recited using musical scales, known as *maqams* in Arabic, and the Taliban themselves sing *taranas* – songs composed in Afghan musical scales. However, they overlook these nuances, and they are mainly opposed to musical instruments."

Since the Taliban's return, the move towards cultural censorship has gradually worsened, said Ahmad Sarmast, who is the founder of the Afghanistan National Institute of Music, an exiled music school now based in Portugal.

Three years after their takeover, the Taliban announced their "vice and virtue laws", which have been internationally condemned by human rights groups and the UN. These put in writing the banning of music, said Sarmast, as well as the restriction of women singing or reading aloud in public. This is in addition to the chilling stipulation that women must not speak or show their faces outside their homes.

Cultural bans have since been extended to the wider creative industries, such as filming and photography. The new morality laws prescribe that news media cannot publish images of living things, and TV stations across the country are gradually being closed and converted to radio stations as a result, according to a report from the London-based news site Afghanistan International.

"It's not just the ban of music or the destruction of musical instruments – it's

It's a direct attack on the cultural heritage of Afghanistan

a direct attack on the cultural heritage of Afghanistan, and on the freedom of expression of the Afghan people," said Sarmast.

His orchestral school, which teaches classical Afghan as well as classical and modern Western music, has been "on the Taliban's hit list" for a decade, →

BELOW: A young man plays a handmade tanbur (a long-necked lute) in Zaranj

ABOVE: Singer-songwriter Elaha Soroor left Afghanistan in 2010, and now lives in the UK

→ he told Index, and endured suicide bombing attempts and targeted attacks even before the group came back into power. Despite the international "whitewashing" of Taliban 2.0, he knew the organisation was "not capable of being changed".

"We knew that when the Taliban came, our days would be over," he said.

In a similar way to Saghar's university department, his music school was "treated like a military barracks" when the Taliban returned. The campus was vandalised, students and faculty were denied entry, property was removed and its bank account was seized.

"Afghanistan was suddenly turned into a silenced nation," said Sarmast.

Musicians who have been granted asylum tend to be those with a public profile and strong international connections, or those from wealthier backgrounds. Others sold everything they could and took up low-paid jobs, such as selling street food, to survive, Sarmast explained.

One female violinist spoke to Index anonymously about her experiences. She was previously a music teacher but now cannot get a job because she doesn't have legitimate qualifications beyond her musical education, which is now worthless.

She is currently in hiding and has had to move house several times to avoid being found out as a former musician. She has applied for asylum in Europe, but hasn't yet been accepted.

"We don't have a peaceful life. We have to be hidden," she said. "No one should know that we used to make music. If the Taliban find out, they will kill us."

Life is particularly treacherous for female musicians. This didn't start when the Taliban came back into power, but it has worsened, says London-based Afghan singer Elaha Soroor. She told Index that gender discrimination from the fallout from the Taliban's previous reign made her situation untenable.

"There was a patriarchy, this system, this way of looking at women's lives – it's always been there," she said. "But the Taliban is the worst form of patriarchy. The foundation was there, but people were changing slowly [after their earlier fall], and things were becoming more normal."

Soroor, who is of the persecuted Hazara ethnic group, was one of the first female musicians to perform in public after the fall of the Taliban in 2000, and appeared on the reality TV show Afghan Star in 2008. She faced death threats, harassment and violence because of her public profile, including from male family members. When an anonymous person uploaded a fake pornographic video of her to YouTube, the violence escalated, and she fled Afghanistan in 2010, seeking asylum in the UK in 2012.

Whilst society was still restrictive, there was more freedom for musical expression then, she said. Bands played at weddings, "music travellers" would walk around the streets with percussion instruments and people loved listening to music.

"You'd go to a taxi [and] everybody's listening to music at a loud volume," she said. "It was mainly Afghan pop music from the '60s and '70s, new music, Bollywood, Turkish, Arabic and Hindustani."

She believes that the Taliban's draconian laws are a way of limiting free thought.

"Musicians, artists, they open up new doors and new ideas. They have this power of entering someone's subconscious. The Taliban are scared of the power of art, because it can spark new ideas in someone's mind, and change their way of thinking," she said.

Now that she's out of the country, she believes it is her role as an exiled musician to help keep Afghan music alive. In October, she released a new female liberation song titled *Naan, Kar, Azadi!* (Bread, Work, Freedom!), which she sings in her mother language, Farsi. It features other exiled female Afghans who have spoken out against the Taliban's oppressive rule, including rapper Sonita Alizadeh. On Instagram, Soroor dedicated the song to "our sisters in Afghanistan as they continue to fight for their rights… in the face of adversity".

"I feel like the artists who are outside Afghanistan… should be more proactive, create more and stay connected with the story of Afghanistan," Soroor said. "So at least, if people cannot produce art inside, we should continue producing it outside and export it there [through the

> No one should know that we used to make music. If the Taliban find out, they will kill us

internet]. So we keep the flame alive."

Cayenna Ponchione-Bailey, who produced Soroor's latest track, is director of performance at Oxford University's St Catherine's College, and an academic specialising in orchestral music in Afghanistan. She is working with exiled Afghan musicians to write the first book on orchestral music in the country.

She says that while there is an "absolute ban on music", its enforcement is likely "uneven". It's possible that, in less policed areas, people still listen to music and "engage in their traditional music practices" at home, but professional music-making has certainly been brought to a standstill, which will have long-term impacts on the country's musical heritage.

"You can't work – there are no weddings, no parties," she told Index. "So you have people's musical knowledge and skill-sets that are probably atrophying. Then they're becoming impoverished because they don't have alternative work opportunities." This has lowered the "social status" of musicians, she said, to historically what it would have been when it was intertwined with "vices" such as alcohol and drug use.

She is particularly concerned about traditional musicians, who she says have been overlooked by European asylum schemes. These have typically given preference to schools making orchestral music – or "Western" music – as they have stronger diplomatic ties with international orchestras, and their students are often better educated with stronger English language skills.

Music made using instruments such as the *rubab*, the *tanbur* and the *dholak* could be lost. She is calling for Germany, which has already established asylum schemes, to set up an Institute of Afghanistan Traditional Music, which could become an international hub for the art form and could help to "potentially get more people out of the country to teach".

Artists who made "modern" music,

ABOVE: Afghans play the dambora at a music festival in Bamyan province in 2017

such as rock and pop, also remain stranded in the country. One singer-songwriter and guitar player spoke to Index anonymously. He taught himself the guitar after practising on his father's *dotar*. His income stream from music has completely stopped. While he sees music "as a way for great social and cultural change, rather than for money making", that too has been curtailed.

Having a public profile as a musician is now "almost equal to signing my death certificate", he said. He has endured threats and physical attacks, and the situation has severely impacted his mental health. "I spend every day with worry and every night with fear, and sometimes I jump from sleep," he said. "The mental problems that have been created for me are sometimes unbearable. I am always worried about being arrested, killed or tortured."

Prior to 2021, he would perform for events like International Women's Day. He hopes that one day girls and women can "study freely and play music, and not be deprived of their basic rights".

"The absence of music and art has caused freedom of expression to disappear, creativity in culture and art to decline, and national and cultural identity to be weakened," he said.

Those who have fled Afghanistan have been torn away from their home country, but are still beating the drum for progress and equality. Sarmast, of the Afghanistan National Institute of Music, says that the international music community must work together to raise awareness of the cultural destruction and "gender apartheid" that is happening, and put pressure on the Taliban to restore human rights, of which he believes access to music is one.

As Afghan musicians live in the shadows, those in exile continue to raise awareness of their plight. But there is a real risk that the rich musical heritage of the country will be forever silenced if the world doesn't continue to campaign for its right to exist. ✖

Sarah Dawood is editor at Index

SPECIAL REPORT ♦ UNSUNG HEROES

The war on drill

Young Black men are disproportionately having their music censored online and criminalised, writes **MACKENZIE ARGENT**

IN JANUARY 2019, there was a landmark case in British legal history – it was the first time someone received a prison sentence for performing a song.

The perpetrators were Brixton duo Skengdo x AM, one of the brightest acts of the burgeoning UK drill scene. They had already been put under surveillance by the police after they and two other members of rap group 410 were handed a gang injunction in 2018. This was in response to a song they released depicting clashes with members of rival crews.

Three young men from those crews were killed that year, but there was no evidence that members of 410 were involved. The Metropolitan Police still classified 410 as a gang, and the injunction prevented them from entering the "rival" SE11 London postcode area, and from performing songs with lyrics that mentioned rival crews.

But at a concert in December 2018, Skengdo x AM broke the injunction. The pair performed one of their more popular songs, Attempted 1.0, which contained lyrics that were regarded by police as inciting violence. Officers discovered videos of the performance online – and in January 2019 the pair were given nine-month prison sentences,

SPECIAL REPORT: UNSUNG HEROES

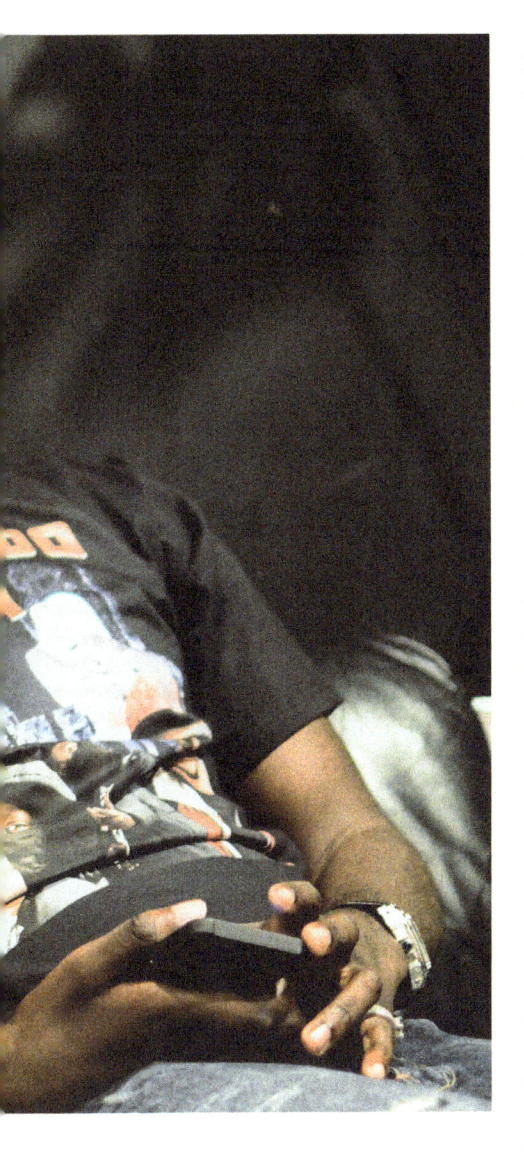

ABOVE: Skengdo x AM backstage at their Greener on the Other Side EP launch at the Ace Hotel, Shoreditch

CREDIT: Finesse Foreva, CC BY-SA 4.0, via Wikimedia Commons

suspended for two years.

In a statement, the Met said that the injunction was breached when "they performed drill music that incited and encouraged violence against rival gang members and then posted it on social media". But it was their fans that shared videos, not them. Shereener Browne, a former barrister for Garden Court Chambers, has spent years working on cases involving young people alleged to be involved in gang or criminal activity. She was shocked by this case, particularly given the pair hadn't posted online themselves.

"So here, they got an order for not doing anything, and then got an order saying that they were in breach of that order for something that they didn't do! Head blown," she told Index.

"So we're just… tearing up Magna Carta – every principle of criminal law is up for grabs. And if it was happening to any other group? We would be marching."

This is a case that Index on Censorship commented on at the time – and it is not the only instance of UK police trying to control the work of drill artists.

One notable case was that of Digga D. In 2018, Digga D (full name Rhys Herbert) was convicted of conspiring to commit violent disorder and ultimately sentenced to a year behind bars. He was also given a criminal behaviour order (CBO) which, alongside having his movements tracked, meant he was required to notify police within 24 hours of uploading music or videos online.

Additionally, the lyrics of his songs had to be verified and authorised by the police to ensure that they did not incite violence. If they did, he could be sent back to prison. These restrictions meant that police essentially had control over his work, and this will continue until 2025. Digga D is one of the most influential drill artists on the scene, but even he is forced to censor his work under police surveillance.

The Met has been scrutinising drill musicians for a while. In 2019, it launched a targeted initiative titled Project Alpha which scoured social media platforms for potential signs of gang activity in posts and videos by young, usually Black, people.

As revealed by The Guardian, the force monitors the activity of young people – primarily young men aged 15 to 21 – online, which it says aims to fight serious violence, identify offenders and assist in removing videos that glorify stabbings and shootings. In many cases, Big Tech is complying, and this policy has led to hundreds of drill music videos being removed from platforms such as YouTube, Instagram and TikTok.

In a Freedom of Information application on Project Alpha, it was revealed that the Met made 682 requests to remove drill songs from streaming platforms between 1 January 2021 and 31 October 2023, with most requests made to YouTube.

Another FOI request found that on YouTube specifically, 654 requests for removal were made between September 2020 and January 2022, and 635 of them were granted.

Browne believes that the claimed attempt to tackle gang violence has become a concerted effort to silence drill artists, and young Black men in particular.

It amounts to systemic racism, she told Index, with the evidence for this being that other genres of music are not censored or surveilled in the same way.

"It creates a culture of fear amongst mainly young, Black men, and it makes them feel even more disenfranchised, marginalised and silenced," she said. "Because if you see your heroes – and I think to a lot of these young men, the drill and rap artists that break through are seen as their heroes – being silenced in that way, it's going to make you angry and frustrated.

"There's this demonisation of an entire generation of young Black people, and it's crushing their self-esteem."

The moral panic surrounding drill music means it has become common →

> There's this demonisation of an entire generation of young Black people, and it's crushing their self-esteem

→ practice for lyrics to be used in court as evidence of criminal activity amongst drill artists. Rapping about crime and violence is often seen as an admission of guilt rather than musical storytelling, and even listening to drill music can be taken as a precursor to violent behaviour.

Art Not Evidence is a campaign group fighting against the criminalisation of drill. Founded a year ago, it has collaborated with musicians and human rights organisations to battle against the use of lyrics – and creative expression more broadly – to unfairly implicate people in criminal charges when there is a lack of real evidence.

Co-founder Elli Brazzill works in the music industry and has spent time at a major record label with some of the biggest names in music. She noticed how the police began to interfere with the work of drill artists signed to the label.

"I started to see the disparities between the way different artists are treated, and what I referred to as a correlation between the growing popularity of certain rap and drill artists

BELOW: Digga D performs live at the Royal Albert Hall on 23 October 2023, with the performance including a fake arrest

What all the other genres are awarded, and rap and drill music are not, is artistic licence

and an increase in police interference and surveillance," she told Index.

One artist who was signed after serving a prison sentence was at risk of further criminal punishment for simply posting online about Black Lives Matter, she claimed.

In founding Art Not Evidence, Brazzill hopes that she can help change presumptions around drill music, from a violent and dangerous genre to a form of therapy and creative expression.

"What all the other genres are awarded, and rap and drill music are not, is artistic licence," she said. "Which is why it comes up in court as autobiographical, as literal, as a confession, as a premeditation to crime."

Music can be a therapeutic tool. According to the charity Youth Music, which conducted a survey of 16 to 24-year-olds last year, nearly three quarters found that listening to, reading or writing musical lyrics enabled them to "process difficult feelings and emotions", whilst half said it helped to reduce feelings of isolation or loneliness.

"That is what these kids need, especially if you're in a community where you don't talk about things," said Brazzill. "I'm 28 now, and I still struggle to talk about my emotions! When you're 15, all you can do is let it out like this. I'm pretty sure every artist would say that that is what it is for them."

Censoring drill music only further ostracises an already-marginalised group, Browne believes. "It's a group of young men who have fallen through the cracks – very often excluded from schools, put into pupil referral units… they're not doing their A-levels, they're not going to university," she said.

"There are very, very few legitimate ways for them to raise themselves [and] lift themselves out of poverty, and this is one of the few ways that they can do that. That's why it's even more cruel for the state to try to shut down those avenues of escape."

Her point is valid. If these young Black people cannot tell the stories and realities of their lives, and they are instead silenced because their retelling is deemed "too violent" or "glorifies gang culture", we are depriving them of a crucial outlet, erasing a core element of modern-day British culture and exacerbating the cycle of poverty and crime.

And inevitably, this can only lead to prison sentences for some young people. Brazzill recalled the poignant words of one drill artist from a recent podcast interview: "You are really angry, and you don't want us to make the music talking about our life. But you don't care if we'll just go back and have to do The Life." ✖

Mackenzie Argent is editorial assistant and the 2024-25 Tim Hetherington fellow at Index

SPECIAL REPORT ♦ UNSUNG HEROES

A force for good

Music has long been used in Bangladesh as a form of liberation and a means for expressing national identity, writes **SALIL TRIPATHI**

ABOVE: Artists react to Sheikh Hasina Wazed's resignation in Dhaka, Bangladesh. A student paints graffiti on a street wall at Dhaka University campus in August 2024

IN 1905, LORD Curzon, the British viceroy in India, decided to divide the province of Bengal into two – East and West. What seemed like an administrative decision had a profoundly political implication. It tore apart a land united by language into two segments – one predominantly Muslim, the other predominantly Hindu.

The move was immensely unpopular. Bengalis rose as one to oppose it and discovered that what united them – their culture and language – was more important than what the British colonial masters were seeking to separate them by – their faith.

One song epitomised the call for a united Bengal at the time – *Dhono Dhanno Pushpo Bhora*, by poet Dwijendralal Ray.

This summer, when Bangladeshis rose against (now-former) Prime Minister Hasina Wazed's increasingly unpopular rule, it was that song many turned to.

Many sang it on the streets and many more made videos with AI-generated images and posted them online before the government cracked down and briefly suspended access to the internet. But Bangladeshis are ingenious people. They found other ways to speak out, including using VPNs to send harrowing images of the terror Hasina's regime had unleashed on the country's people.

Music matters to every society, but in Bangladesh in particular music has played a prominent role in various struggles for freedom. Ray's song was among the many that roused the people at the start of the 20th century, and by 1911 the British annulled the partition, reuniting the province.

But the British had sown divisive seeds, and by the 1930s there were loud calls for dividing India. Muslims sought a homeland for themselves and began campaigning for a separate nation.

In 1947, when the British finally left, the country was divided into a Hindu-majority India and a Muslim-majority Pakistan, which itself was divided into two – the Punjabi-dominated west and the Bengali-dominated east.

Artificially uniting a nation purely by religion would not hold, particularly after the politically dominant west Pakistan refused to give Bengali the status of a national language.

LEFT: Bengali poet, playwright and musician, Dwijendralal Ray (1863 - 1913)

A language movement emerged in 1952, with music being dominant as well. Songs such as Abdul Gaffar Chowdhury's *Amar Bhaier Rokte Rangano Ekushe February* (My Brothers' Blood Splattered 21 February) and Gazi Mazharul Anwar's *Joy Bangla, Banglar Joy* (Hail Bengal, Victory to Bengal) remain symbols of rebellion.

The UN designated 21 February as International Mother Language Day in 1999 as a tribute to Bangladesh's language movement.

It commemorates the date in February 1952 when Pakistani troops killed several students seeking an official status for the Bengali language. Conflict was inevitable and, after a brutal civil war, east Pakistan separated from the west, becoming the independent nation Bangladesh in 1971.

But not without music.

As the film *Muktir Gaan* (Song of Freedom) – directed by the late Tareque Masud and his wife Catherine – shows, music plays an extremely important part in forging a national identity and unity of purpose.

Bangladesh was still part of Pakistan when the country went to the polls in →

LEFT: In a protest against Sheikh Hasina Wazed in Dhaka, people damage a painted portrait of the former prime minister in August 2024

→ 1970. The Bengali nationalist party, Awami League, won an overwhelming majority in the east, with sufficient seats to form a government.

But military rulers in the west refused to cede power and engaged Awami League's leader, Mujibur Rahman, in endless talks as it gathered forces for a military crackdown.

In March 1971, the talks were called off and the Pakistani army massacred hundreds of thousands of civilians in order to intimidate the Bengalis.

But the Bengalis, who would soon become Bangladeshis, resisted fiercely, aided and abetted by India. And while the loss of lives was incalculable, the Pakistani forces were defeated by December that year and surrendered. Bangladesh became free.

Throughout that period, music played an important role in keeping Bangladeshi spirits up. Not only that, the coded messages India sent to Bangladeshi guerrillas – about when they should attack and when they should move – were through clandestine radio networks and played through familiar songs from poets such as Rabindranath Tagore. These messages outwardly seemed harmless but were nudges to the young warriors – the *Mukti Bahini* – to act.

Meanwhile, the Bangladesh *Mukti Sangrami Shilpi Sangstha* (Bangladesh Liberation Art Organisation) travelled to refugee camps in India to perform patriotic songs and stage puppet shows and plays to inspire the dispossessed people and those itching to return to Bangladesh to fight.

It was hardly surprising that when the Bangladeshi youth rose against Hasina's regime this year they turned to the arts. There has been an outpouring of astonishingly moving and rich street art all over Dhaka during the summer. And there has been music.

For many Bangladeshis, Hasina's rule represented a dark period. While official biographies claim she won several elections, the fact remains that she really won only twice – in 1991, in a coalition, and then in 2008.

While she claimed to win the three elections that followed, those were rigged – and, in at least two instances, most opposition parties boycotted them. When they did take part, they withdrew candidates before polling closed when they realised how much intimidation and rigging was going on.

Hasina was able to remain in power for two reasons – she convinced the world that she was able to tackle Islamic extremism, and she retained steadfast support from Bangladesh's influential neighbour, India.

But, ultimately, accusations of corruption and human rights abuses, a crackdown on dissidents, the disappearance of political opponents and control over free speech and the internet – alongside growing economic strife and rising unemployment – led to a tipping point.

And in that dark night, Bangladeshis began to sing: "In the dark times, will there also be singing? Yes, there will also be singing. About the dark times."

That famous verse from Bertolt Brecht was shared online and through text messages, and videos were created using patriotic songs such as Ray's *Janmobhoomi* and Bangladesh's national anthem, *Amar Sonar Bangla*, which was written by the Bengali Nobel laureate Rabindranath Tagore (the only poet to have written the national anthem for two countries, India and Bangladesh).

Bangladeshis sang across the nation, drowning the government's propaganda with art. Hannan, a rapper, created the hip hop anthem *Awaaz Utha* (Raise Your Voice) which got more than two million views on YouTube before you could say "Bangladesh".

It pleads to Bangladeshis to speak out against Hasina's rule and begins with

> Music matters to every society, but in Bangladesh in particular music has played a prominent role in various struggles for freedom

SPECIAL REPORT: UNSUNG HEROES

the voice of Hasina's father, Mujibur Rahman (Bangladesh's founding father), delivering a historic speech in which he calls for Bangladeshis' freedom.

The song reminds people of the pain and sacrifices Bangladeshis had to bear because Mujibur's daughter had turned authoritarian. A translation reads:

*"We don't come from any league nor from any party,
We are taking to the streets, with a shroud on our heads we shall bring you down,
I'm a martyr, I'll smile and take the bullet from the barrel,
Silence the students' voice, come the commands from the party…"*

Unsurprisingly, in July, Hannan was arrested and it led to a public outcry. Other rappers took over the mantle and subversive hip hop spread like wildfire.

Shezan's Kotha Ko (Speak Up) became an anthem and had an electrifying impact, reminding listeners of the sacrifices of 1952 and 1971, and linking those with the present.

*"52 and 24 – where's the difference? Speak up!
The country is free, so what's the trouble? Speak up!
My brothers and sisters die in the street, where's your effort? Speak up!"*

The track represented outrage over Hasina's rule. In an unguarded moment, she had called the students opposing her "*razakars*", a particularly grave insult in Bangladesh. It is the term used for those who collaborated with Pakistani armed forces in 1971. Shezan's song taunted Hasina: "One Shezan may die, and a lakh [100,000] Shezans will say, speak up!" The track ends abruptly with the sound of sniper fire.

Then there is the guitar-slinging

RIGHT: Bangladeshi rapper Hannan Hossain Shimul ("Hannan") was arrested in July

It was hardly surprising that when the Bangladeshi youth rose against Hasina's regime this year, they would turn to the arts

Farzana Wahid, or Shayan, whose music has been the voice of resistance for some time. She posts songs and poems on social media. In the song *Bhoy Banglay* (Fear in Bangla), which she wrote in 2019 as a tribute to Abrar Fahad, a student who had been killed, she challenges the nation's political leadership.

Then there are songs such as Gogon Sakib's *Chakri* (Job), which uses humour to tackle social issues like unemployment – in particular, the movement against government-introduced recruitment quotas. Chakri outlines the story of a man struggling to survive without a job.

*"With a wound on my chest like a cuckoo,
I count the days endlessly in the hope of getting a job,
If my uncle was a somebody, I would've landed the job,
Now I want to eat up my certificates…"*

The words of the brave Parsha Purnee deliver punches to hurt complacent Bangladeshis. "You and I live on, standing atop corpses," Purnee sings, mocking Dhaka residents who praised the metro rail introduced during the Hasina years.

At the end of *Cholo Bhule Jai* (Let Us Forget), Purnee sang:

*"Let the elites hold on to power, clinging to their thrones
I shall return with another song if I am alive yet!"*

Music has flowed through Bengali veins and Bangladeshi blood. Any government that attempts to stop it would be stupid. ✖

Salil Tripathi is Index's South Asia contributing editor. His book on Bangladesh, The Colonel Who Would Not Repent, recounts the nation's history

SPECIAL REPORT ♦ UNSUNG HEROES

Georgia on my mind

As the country's divisive new "foreign agent law" is put into action, **JP O'MALLEY** explores how musicians are standing up to the conservative establishment

RESO KIKNADZE HAS a colourful musical career that stretches back five decades.

He played saxophone in the Georgian TV Big Band and sang in a choir that made traditional music popular again during the 1980s in Georgia, a small transcontinental nation at the crossroads between Europe and Asia.

In 1991, Kiknadze left the country and emigrated to Lübeck in northern Germany to study composition and electro-acoustic music. That December, Mikhail Gorbachev, the last leader of the Soviet Union, resigned and the union was formally dissolved. Georgia had been a member, but its secession had happened earlier that year.

The date the parliament chose to formally mark the country's independence – 9 April 1991 – was not coincidental. It was exactly two years after the tragedy of 1989, also known as the massacre of Tbilisi, when the Soviet army killed 21 civilians who had been taking part in a peaceful pro-independence demonstration on Rustaveli Avenue in Georgia's capital.

Kiknadze, who returned to Georgia in 2008 and is now a professor and head of the music centre at Ilia State University in Tbilisi, remembers that brutality. Today, state-sanctioned violence against peaceful street protestors is happening again.

Many of his students regularly attend street demonstrations "because they feel that freedom of speech and freedom of expression is being taken away from them", he told Index.

In April, Kiknadze joined them and other musicians in those protests in Tbilisi, which continued into May. "We were breathing in this terrible [tear] gas, and the [police] were using water cannons against us," the 64-year-old musician said. "Two artists I know were sadistically beaten by the police."

Those protests happened after Georgian Dream, a populist party which has been in power since 2012, announced that it was resurrecting its "foreign agent law".

In March 2023, a previous version of the law was defeated by a wave of street protests.

But in May 2024, parliament finally passed an updated version of the law, which requires non-governmental organisations and independent media in Georgia that receive more than 20% of their funding from foreign donors to register as organisations "bearing the interests of a foreign power".

Many Georgians refer to it as "the Russian law", as it's loosely modelled on legislation the Kremlin passed in 2012.

In 2015, Georgia joined the EU's Creative Europe Programme, which provides funding for Georgian artists to attend residencies in Europe, collaborate internationally and receive grants for their work.

"This funding has been crucial for promoting Georgian culture, music and art on international platforms," said Mariam Otarashvili, a spokesperson for Mutant Radio, which broadcasts educational shows and live performances of Georgian musicians, artists and DJs. "As an NGO, Mutant Radio has chosen not to register as 'foreign agents' and so we will be forced to close."

She claims Georgian Dream is weaponising culture for its own conservative political agenda, and said: "There is a resemblance here to the Soviet strategy of controlling public expression – where theatres, literature and artistic spaces were monitored and censored to ensure they aligned with state ideology."

Rezo Glonti, a Tbilisi-based sound artist and electronic music producer, said Georgian Dream did not have any ideology per se. "All they want is a way to stay [in] power," he explained. "In this sense, their model is basically

CREDIT: (band) Taiko Skripnichenko / M.K. / Outer Emigrant

LEFT: Musician and producer Gvantsa Uma Japaridze

SPECIAL REPORT: UNSUNG HEROES

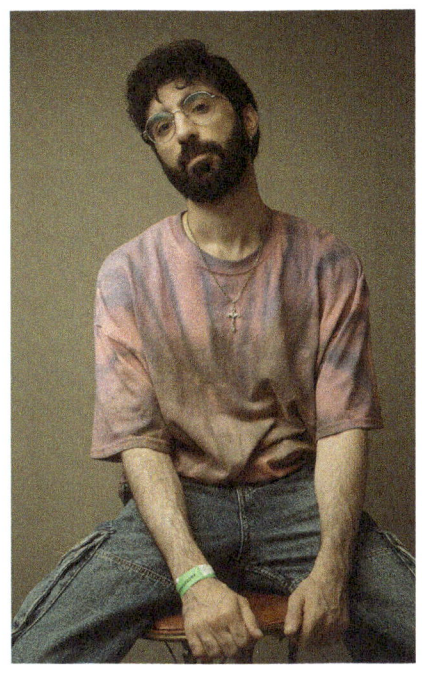

ABOVE: Musicians in Georgia have spoken out about the government and partaken in political protest. From left to right: Gvantsa Uma Japaridze; Dato of Bedford Falls; performances for the media platform, Mutant Radio

Putin's Russia."

The 38-year-old also participated in Tbilisi's demonstrations in the spring.

"This year, the police seemed more prepared and were noticeably more aggressive – they wore balaclavas and were extremely intimidating," he said. "Some of my musician friends were captured by the police, brutally beaten up, then taken into custody for 48 hours where they were interrogated."

Glonti also mentioned how many of the protesters "received phone calls from unknown numbers. These callers threatened more violence if the protests continued".

Many musicians, artists, journalists and members of opposition parties have received similar anonymous phone calls "with threats and intimidation" over the past few months, said Guram Imnadze, director of the democracy and justice programme at the Social Justice Centre, a Tbilisi-based human rights NGO.

He also spoke about the "family values and the protection of minors" law that the parliament approved in September, which forbids Georgian media from freely broadcasting any information related to LGBTQ+ issues.

"This law restricts legal rights for any sexual minority groups," he said. "It also impacts on freedom of expression for musicians, who can be punished for representing homosexuality in a positive manner."

Gvantsa Japaridze, an experimental artist whose music combines natural sounds with various instruments, said: "This law is yet another step by Georgian Dream to spread homophobic influence in Georgia and to suppress free artistic expression.

"It denies LGBTQ+ people basic human rights and refuses to grant them equality, so many people from the LGBTQ+ community are now planning to leave Georgia."

She said many female musicians "felt threatened at the street protests in Tbilisi last spring, especially those who were called to appear in court over their views".

Political street protests in Tbilisi continue. The latest wave began after the election on 26 October, when Georgian Dream claimed victory with 54% of the vote.

The opposition, which includes Georgia's pro-European president, Salome Zourabichvili, has refused to recognise the validity of the results, alleging massive fraud, vote rigging, intimidation and Russian interference. This is a view that Japaridze shares.

"Georgian Dream stole the election →

Creatives believe that Georgian Dream is weaponising culture for its own conservative political agenda

ABOVE: A woman holds the Georgian flag during a protest against alleged violations in a recent parliamentary election in Tbilisi

→ with the help of Russia," she said.

Glonti also claimed there was intimidation leading up to, and during, the election.

"These intimidation tactics generally happen in rural regions, where many people get their information from state-run television," he said.

And Kiknadze added: "Georgian Dream collects many of its votes through intimidation and bribery. People from poorer socio-economic backgrounds are very easy to intimidate and bribe and this [is] how our government collects many of its votes."

Georgia applied for EU membership in March 2022, shortly after Russia invaded Ukraine, and was granted candidate status in December 2023.

Index interviewed a wide cohort of Tbilisi-based musicians, who all spoke about the benefits of the country joining the EU.

In a statement, indie rock band Loudspeakers said: "Georgia has always been part of European civilisation, and our future belongs with Europe and the European Union. We believe our relentless struggle will soon turn into victory."

But not all musicians share that enthusiasm. Many speak about an uninspiring protest movement which lacks energy, direction, a clear goal and, most importantly, leadership.

"The problem in Georgia right now is that there is nobody in the opposition that people can trust," said Glonti.

Dato is the lead singer in indie rock band Bedford Falls. "The enthusiasm to keep protesting is dying out," he said. "We already protested in April and May against this Russian law, but there was no compromise from our government on it. We are being ignored. There is no real plan here."

The Georgian-Swiss composer and performer Alexandre Kordzaia, aka Kordz, echoed that view. He said that "as time goes on, the political opposition in this country just becomes weaker and weaker".

Still, a glimmer of hope remains. "There was great music made in the Soviet Union where extreme political conditions often prevailed," he said. "Ultimately, the quality of art will not be affected. We will make music no matter what happens." ✖

JP O' Malley is a freelance journalist based in London

> Some of my musician friends were captured by the police, brutally beaten up, then taken into custody for 48 hours, where they were interrogated

SPECIAL REPORT ◆ UNSUNG HEROES

Murdered for music

In Turkey, musicians are being targeted for their political views, for their Kurdish background or for simply performing, writes **KAYA GENÇ**

ON 2 MAY 2023, Cihan Aymaz, a 30-year-old Kurdish musician, sang a song with his *saz* (a traditional folk string instrument) by the Kadıköy ferry pier, a seaside hub in Istanbul's Asian side. Hundreds walked past him on their way to the ferry during the day: he had performed there for the past two years. Some of those who listened to his songs paid Aymaz for his music in solidarity.

Mehmet Caymaz felt differently. When he requested that Aymaz play the nationalistic song *Ölürüm Türkiyem* (I'll Die For You, Turkey), Caymaz considered it an order. But Aymaz refused Caymaz's request. Infuriated, Caymaz pulled out a knife and stabbed the musician repeatedly, including in the heart. Aymaz fell into the water. To flee the surrounding crowd, Caymaz also jumped in and tried to swim away. The coastguard fished him out of the water, and detained and handcuffed him.

In January that year, Aymaz had gone to court for singing a song he had adapted from Aşık Mahzuni Şerif, an Alevi folk musician and composer. Since the 16th century, some orthodox Sunnis have considered Alevis as rebels and dissidents. The song also has lyrics highlighting Turkey's economic collapse. Aymaz's family believes his killing by the Kadıköy pier, in front of thousands of pedestrians, was a political or racially-motivated murder rather than simply due to a burst of rage. →

BELOW: A man plays a daf, a flat handheld drum, during Newroz celebrations in Istanbul. Newroz marks Kurdish new year and is a festival of music and dance

CREDIT: AP Photo / Francisco Seco / Alamy

→ "I told him so many times not to voice his political views, that people would murder him for doing so, but he didn't listen to me," his mother, Birgül Aymaz, told the Turkish press.

A day after the murder, musicians left guitars, hand drums, tambourines and clarions at the spot where Aymaz was killed to commemorate him. In July 2024, Caymaz was sentenced to life imprisonment.

The murder was part of a pattern of animosity and violence against Turkey's musicians over the past half-decade. And that was just one of the issues they had to contend with.

When Covid-19 struck in 2020, musicians lost the opportunity to perform in public venues; after the partial reopening of the country, they had to accept smaller concert royalties because of reduced demand, and many were forced to change careers.

Jehan İstiklal Barbur, a Turkish singer-songwriter of Arab Christian descent, told BBC's Turkish edition she was making and selling jewellery to make ends meet.

Many independent concert and theatre venues reported not receiving any financial support from Turkey's culture ministry during the pandemic, and ultimately went bankrupt. Between July 2021 and May 2022, the government banned live music after midnight.

Harun Tekin, lead singer of the band Mor ve Ötesi, wrote on social media that the music sector was going through difficult times: "Dear people, Turkey's concert and music industries are about to end, be aware of this."

Musicians have always been subjected to violence and bullying

Onur Şener was another musician trying to navigate this atmosphere and make ends meet. The 45-year-old, who had a daughter, was singing in a venue in the capital Ankara on 2 October 2022 when he was attacked with beer glasses and had his throat cut. He was attacked after he refused to sing a song he had been asked for.

In July 2023, İlker Karakaş and Ali Gündüz were each given 25 years in prison for the murder. They had worked for the Ministry of Labour and Social Security since 2012. Şener's death changed the life of Naim Dilmener, a music critic and historian, who quit DJ-ing after the murder. Dilmener spoke to Index about his experiences.

He had DJ-ed in Turkey for years, but around the time of Şener's murder he noticed a change. He was in a venue in southern Turkey when a group of people went to the DJ booth and stopped him from playing a Kurdish song by the singer Aynur. He said the venue owner approached him and told him: "Stop this song immediately, or there will be chaos." Dilmener complied.

Another time, he says he was playing an Aynur song at a party for the Antalya International Film Festival when the venue owner cut the power. "The party ended there," he said. "You see, I don't learn from past mistakes!"

After these incidents, Dilmener sat down and told himself: "Stop this job before something happens to you." He stopped DJ-ing. Dilmener explained how Şener's death was linked with intolerance in Turkish society.

"Some people don't want to be rejected under any circumstances," he said. "They see themselves as the owners of that venue. Since they are there and have paid, or will pay, they think musicians should be at their disposal and fulfil all their wishes: singers, players, DJs, the whole set." Money has "bankrupted humanity" in Turkey, he added.

In a country where even DJ-ing can be dangerous, musicians must be extra brave when going on stage to sing to big

ABOVE: A musical performance takes place at a peaceful protest in Istanbul in 2013. The protest was met with tear gas and water cannons by Turkish police

crowds. When Suavi, an Ankara-based performer of Turkish folk music, played at a concert organised by Istanbul's Beykoz district council on 19 August 2024, a group of nationalists raided

SPECIAL REPORT: UNSUNG HEROES

the concert, shouting far-right slogans and accusing Suavi of being a terrorist. Unfazed, Suavi continued singing. A fortnight later, the far-right group convinced a council in Konya to cancel his next concert because "it didn't align with national sensitivities".

Suavi told Index that the attack on his concert and the subsequent cancellation "cannot be evaluated independently of how the government handles the Kurdish reality". The objective, Suavi said, was to "instil fear in all opposition artists through me and to gain ground for fascists".

Violence against musicians in Turkey has a long history that predates these incidents. "Musicians have always been subjected to violence and bullying, regardless of the violence that has increased in recent years due to the economic crisis," Mehmet Tez told Index.

The music columnist for the daily newspaper Milliyet, Tez believes people in Turkey "have always been violent towards musicians, especially in small places". He added: "I think male-dominated culture and the complexes that come with it come into play at some point."

CREDIT: Claudia Wiens / Alamy

> Leftists and dissidents in general have always been labelled as harmful in our country

Tez worked as a musician in bars and clubs during his university years. "I've been through many things," he said of his musical youth. "Even though we worked in relatively civilised places, we were threatened with guns on the table because we didn't play a request. If someone like me, who has been doing this job for a limited time, has stories like these, think about [what professionals have been through]. This is an issue that shouldn't be underestimated."

Tez wasn't surprised at the killing of Şener. "Unfortunately, people always take these kinds of issues personally," he said.

Dilmener said that despite attempts to hide the political context of the violence, the killings have exposed Turkish politicians' resentment of free thought. "They pretend to be extremely liberal and democratic or try to appear so, but it snows on their image when such incidents come to the agenda. For this reason, they do not want it to be heard, known and spread," he said.

Dilmener, who is 68, also pointed to broader patterns in Turkey that indicate violence towards musicians. "Leftists and dissidents in general have always been labelled as harmful in our country, and efforts have always been made to put spokes in their wheels," he said.

He recalled the 12 September 1980 coup, when prominent pop stars Şanar Yurdatapan, Melike Demirağ and Cem Karaca had to flee. "[They] all went abroad, thinking they would be tried and imprisoned, and they lived in exile for years," he said.

The assaults on Turkey's musicians are part of a broader culture war in the country. "On the one hand, there is the oppression of the government, and on the other hand the brutal force, violent actions and sometimes even threats with weapons from supporters who are more royalist than the king," Dilmener said. "It's all so clear. Those who do not side with the government have been through a lot. They have been left unemployed, and their movements have been restricted. On top of that, they are beaten, even killed."

The silver lining of the latest wave of violence is the solidarity it ignited among musicians. Ankara's mayor, Mansur Yavaş, organised a solidarity concert for Şener's family in 2022.

He wrote on social media: "We are experiencing the pain of musician Onur Şener, who was taken from life yesterday. At the request of his artist friends, we will organise a concert together for Onur and donate the income to his family. We will keep his memory alive and will always be against tyranny."

On 2 November that year, a symphony orchestra and a group of musicians sang songs to support Şener's family. In December, Şener's schoolmates from TED College, where he graduated, went to Çayyolu Neighbourhood to plant the Onur Şener Memorial Forest.

While news about attacks against musicians in venues where patrons pay for entry horrify the public, the treatment of street musicians is under-reported. Tez, the music writer, said they "are much more vulnerable and threatened than musicians playing in venues".

He added: "The murder by the Kadıköy pier was, unfortunately, the most obvious proof of this situation. The problem of violence against musicians is, of course, a part of the general violence in society, but it deserves to be addressed separately."

There are probably numerous other incidents against musicians in Turkey but the public knows only about the ones that result in deaths. Most likely, Tez said, "in the eyes of the authorities", violence against musicians is "not important enough to be addressed separately".

Suavi, the assaulted singer, said he was surprised by people's support "for me and against this disgusting plot". He praised Özgür Özel, the leader of Turkey's main opposition party, the CHP, for defending him. "His acknowledgment of the attack and clear attitude were crucial for not only me but all opposition artists," Suavi said. "People saw the outcome of organised action and how effective that can be."

But he also issued a warning: "This is not just an issue about me. Racist attacks, from targeting musicians in the middle of the street because they sing Kurdish songs to killing people because they did not play the song someone wanted at any entertainment venue, can be solved only as a whole within the framework of the democracy problem. If we're going to live in peace in this country and break these and similar attacks, and gradually create a free country, we have to do this together."

Melis Danişmend, a singer who recently wrote a book about returning to live at her parents' house following the collapse of Istanbul's concert scene in the early 2020s, told Index she feared for her future as a musician in the country.

"We have become a society that lives with anger, is raised with anger and feeds on anger," she said. "The fact that musicians are killed for not playing a requested song shows how sad our situation is.

"I long for the days when the logic of 'If you don't do what I want, I will do what I want' is over and when people respect the law and don't harm musicians or anyone." ✖

Kaya Genç is a novelist, journalist and a contributing editor for Index based in Istanbul

SPECIAL REPORT ♦ UNSUNG HEROES

A Black woman who dared to rock

MALU HALASA speaks to singer-songwriter and bass player **FELICE ROSSER** to explore how Black female voices have largely been excluded from the rock and punk scene

ABOVE: Felice Rosser of the band Faith broke boundaries in rock music in the 1980s

IT'S EASY TO take popular music as a fait accompli. Rock is seen as the preserve of mainly white men, whilst reggae, rap, soul and jazz are Black music. Once algorithms take over music – or, rather, direct its consumption – music becomes another echo chamber. How many Black rockers show up on Apple Music's Rock Classics playlist, for instance? Where is the proto punk band Death, from Detroit, who had an epiphany after seeing Alice Cooper? Or Pure Hell from Philadelphia, a glam rock band in the mould of the New York Dolls?

Playlists determined by chart positions and record sales mean the tastes of the people who rely on them become calcified. In the case of classic rock playlists, the bands are almost entirely white and male. Do Black women's voices and songs have a shot at creating popular music? Or is it a self-fulfilling loop that reflects the inherent racism and misogyny of record executives and/or musical gatekeepers, which stifle diversity and inclusion in popular songs?

History proves illuminating. Despite the massive success of Billie Jean and Beat It from Michael Jackson's Thriller LP, MTV still had to be convinced to play Black music in the early 1980s. It may have been white rocker Eddie Van Halen's whining guitar on Beat It that won it airtime.

By then, African-American inventors of rock'n'roll such as Chuck Berry and Little Richard had been written out of the history of the music they'd created. There was no better proof of rock's whitening than the interview Rolling Stone's editor and founder Jann Wenner gave to The New York Times for his 2023 memoir of musical greats, The Masters. Wenner's dismissive bigoted and chauvinistic comments against Black and women musicians prompted the Rock and Roll Hall of Fame to drop him from its board.

Racial dimensions in the selling and promotion of music goes as far back as the 19th century, according to Karl Hagstrom Miller's Segregating Sound: Inventing Folk and Pop Music in the Age of Jim Crow. He writes that "the terms highbrow and lowbrow … were borrowed from the racist pseudoscience of phrenology which posited that racial types and intelligence could be determined through cranial measurements". In the early 20th century, records directly marketed at and sold to Black audiences and hillbilly/folk recordings released on wholly white labels laid the groundwork for industry attitudes today.

The 1960s folk revival reinforced notions of authenticity and primitivism →

> In the case of classic rock playlists, the bands are almost entirely white and male. Do Black women's voices and songs have a shot at creating popular music?

CREDIT: Caroline Conejero

→ in its championing of the blues. Soul was considered Black, whilst rock, the inheritor of rock'n'roll, was white – except for the anomaly of Jimi Hendrix.

The 1970s emerged as a fertile period for an explosion of independent music, from Philly soul to disco, punk and new wave, which brought with it a new diversity of people to the dancefloors. However, by that decade's end, the ugly face of white rock's fandom revealed itself. Rolling Stone critic Dave Marsh slammed the riot and the burning of disco records at Chicago's Comiskey Park in 1979 as a wider "racist and sexist" attack on gay, Black and Latino people. I was an intern at the magazine at the time, and spent my nights in New York's downtown clubs, listening to punk, reggae, disco and hip hop, much like my Black girlfriend, Felice Rosser. She was then working at CBS Records and playing bass, with an eye on forming her first band.

More than a decade later, she and her band Faith belonged to the Black Rock Coalition, a movement of musicians, critics and activists combating racist stereotypes in rock. Faith's live shows were causing quite a stir and the major record companies were circling. In his history of the BRC, The Wire's music

People were going crazy over Faith in the clubs… but the record executives just couldn't see past a 6ft woman playing bass and singing

critic Michael A Gonzales quotes BRC's conceptual thinker, writer Greg Tate: "People were going crazy over Faith in the clubs ... but the record executives just couldn't see past a 6ft woman playing bass and singing ... All these years later ... when it comes to rock and roll, it's still a white male discussion."

This attitude barred Rosser from contemporary music's most popular, macho genre. She recalls how record companies came up to "the two male members of early Faith" during shows and tried "to talk business, and they'd say, 'No, she's the leader, you have to talk to her'. I feel that sexism had a big part of what happened to Faith then".

There have also been pressures on Black musicians to be better than their white counterparts. "They have to be virtuosos," she said. She cites bassist and poet Meshell Ndegeocello, then signed to Madonna's Maverick label,

and guitarist Vernon Reid of another BRC band, Living Colour. They were "introduced" to the music industry by Mick Jagger of the Rolling Stones.

For some, the Rolling Stones, among many others, were at the forefront of the white wave that co-opted Black music and effectively erased rock's Black originators. In her seminal 1973 essay Ripping Off Black Music, Pulitzer-Prize winning critic Margo Jefferson perceived the mimicking of Black styles and attitudes by white musicians through the prism of 19th century minstrelsy. She wrote: "Black music, and with it the private Black self, were suddenly grossly public – tossed onstage, dressed in clown white and bandied about with a gleeful arrogance that just yesterday had chosen to ignore and condescend."

However, for Rosser, growing up in Detroit, the English invasion into blues was where she learned about the original bluesmen in the musically segregated landscape of the 1960s. She recalled: "Motown was trying to get away from the blues. They wanted to make pop music that could be played on AM radio that would be acceptable to broad American culture. It took the English guys to [bring back that history]."

Fleetwood Mac with Peter Green had come out of England as a blues band, but "by the time Lindsay Buckingham and Stevie Nicks joined – not to take away from the great songs they wrote – and the Eagles had their commercial success, the Black roots of rock had

LEFT: Rosser recalls how record companies came up to "the two male members of early Faith" during shows, rather than her, and tried to "talk business"

faded away", Rosser added.

When Rosser and I were in Detroit together, she talked us past the security guard and got us into the now-defunct Michigan Palace. Torn bits of curtain hung from an enormous stage where concerts by Iggy Pop and the Stooges, and the New York Dolls made deep and lasting impressions on her. Unlike today's internet playlists, which turn listeners into isolated consumers, bands coming to Detroit unified a generation, like the anti-Vietnam War movement.

Of our group of friends from Barnard and Columbia colleges, Rosser was the first one to move to downtown New York. The artist Jean-Michel Basquiat and the novelist Jennifer Jazz – whose debut novel, Spill Ink on It, was about their punk days together – shared a couch in Rosser's apartment on First Avenue. Basquiat then was out on the streets as the graffiti artist "Samo", and heroin-shooting galleries dotted the Lower East Side. Despite its bohemianism, there was old-fashioned racism in the iconic punk club CBGB and within the music business, which the music critic Lester Bangs recounted in his essay The White Noise Supremacists. A female industry figure once told him: "I liked them so much better when they were just Negroes."

Although novelist and editor Kaitlyn Greenidge has described Rosser as "a Black punk pioneer", at a recent photographic exhibition of the old days the musician saw no Black punks in the pictures.

"I feel like a lot of people never even saw us," she said. "They don't even know that Black people were there … I never thought it was odd to be [in the clubs] because everybody else who was there liked this odd, weird stuff, too, so that united us." Reggae, she added, was another unifying force: "At the reggae shows, you'd see white, Black, all kinds of people."

Over the years there have been many iterations of Rosser's original band. The current one, FaithNYC, plays a signature fusion of the musical styles – from rock and reggae to punk and soul – that have shaped her life in music. I introduced her to Justin Adams, Robert Plant's guitarist who'd played with Sinéad O'Connor. Rosser and Adams, together with percussionist Finley Hunt, went into the studio for three tracks and came out with nine. FaithNYC's new LP, Love Is a Wish Away, was released in November on Good Deeds Music.

In his review of the LP for The Wire, Gonzales describes Rosser's voice as having "the texture of whiskey and honey and a chameleon-like versatility". He likens some of Adams's guitar licks to those of Chic's Nile Rodgers. The LP's title single has earned praise from filmmaker Jim Jarmusch and critics Vivian Goldman and Lucy Sante. Drummer Chris Frantz, of Talking Heads and Tom Tom Club, calls the record "a powerful groove and force for good in these troubled times".

This year, Rosser watched another Black woman (this time on the political stage) attempt to smash through the cultural and social barriers that hold back African Americans, and she is adamant about her message. Her music is "the freedom of a Black woman to express herself amidst all the subtle – and not so subtle – rules about who and what a Black woman should be, do, say and feel in American society". ✖

Malu Halasa is an author, editor and journalist, and was one of the first people to write about rap in the UK

ABOVE: Rosser believes her music gives her the "freedom to express herself" amid preconceptions around how Black women should act in American society

SPECIAL REPORT ♦ UNSUNG HEROES

Fear the butterfly

KATIE DANCEY-DOWNS interviews Iranian singer-songwriter **GOLAZIN ARDESTANI** on fleeing persecution, fighting for women's rights and turning personal struggles into a collective movement

IN AROUND 2009, Golazin Ardestani was preparing to go on stage in Tehran. The venue was sold out. She and her university classmates had been through months of rehearsals for their traditional concert and had followed all the rules: they had their songs cleared by the Ministry of Culture and Islamic Guidance, the lead singer was male, the musicians would be seated on the floor and everyone was dressed appropriately, including the correct hijab protocols. And yet, as Ardestani – who goes by the stage name Gola – walked towards the stage, she was told: "No, you can't perform with them. No female musician can go on stage tonight."

She stood at the side of the stage and watched her friends perform without her, clutching the formal permission papers which should have allowed her to sing, and which had been wilfully ignored. This is just one of the heartbreaking memories she has of being a female musician in Iran.

A few years later, Ardestani left Iran for good. Now in her 30s, she is based between Europe and the USA, where she creates music that speaks out against the regime. In 2018, she founded her own record label, Zan Recordings, so that she could finally release music on her own terms.

Ardestani was born in Isfahan, in Iran. She taught herself to yodel as a child and grew up in a house filled with a mix of the traditional Persian music favoured by her parents, and the Iranian and Western pop smuggled in by her older siblings, whose musical preferences were inspired by their desire for freedom.

"My teenage years were full of those stolen moments listening to forbidden songs on satellite," she told Index over email. "Music, and especially female performers, gave me a sense of freedom that was completely absent on our heavily censored government TV."

Growing up, Gola had never seen a woman on an Iranian stage. At age 19, fed up with trying to conform to traditional norms and still being prevented from singing, she joined some friends and a group of three sisters to create Iran's first girl band, Orchid.

They wanted to challenge the narrative of female singers being "provocative", and to resist patriarchal and authoritarian forces. Behind their music was a deep understanding of the history of Iranian music from before the Islamic revolution of 1979, when female singers like Googoosh and Qamar-ol-Moluk Vaziri had been celebrated and were free to perform to mixed audiences.

Orchid was only allowed to perform for female audiences, who had to remain seated. Gestures or movements that could be interpreted as dancing were strictly forbidden. The performers themselves had to avoid showing emotion on stage.

"There were female morality police at the end of each row, watching us and the audience," Ardestani recalled.

The memory of those performances, in front of thousands of women, is still vivid.

"It was such a powerful experience that I remember making a promise to myself that night: that I would sing, I would sing solo, and I would one day sing for a mixed audience," she said. "I held onto this vision of a day when our fathers, brothers, husbands and sons could feel proud of the women on stage."

Whilst in Iran, Ardestani was arrested three times by the morality police, experiences which she said shaped her music and her determination to keep fighting.

The first occasion was when she was just 16, when she was arrested because her hijab wasn't covering the front of her hair. She sat terrified in a cell and sang to distract herself. A woman shouted at her: "Shut up, close your mouth, shut your ugly voice!"

The last time she was arrested was particularly brutal and was due to the clothes she was wearing. "As they were about to push me into the van, I put on my fighting face, but chaos quickly ensued," she said. A crowd began to form, and she hit something hard, breaking her arm. With the situation out of control, the police's superior told her to go home in a taxi.

"All of this because of my ripped jeans, even though I was wearing a long manto [overcoat] and a scarf covering my hair."

Ardestani considers herself lucky to have escaped alive. Under similar circumstances, Mahsa "Jina" Amini died in custody in September 2022, the moment that sparked the Woman, Life, Freedom uprising.

Before leaving Iran in 2011 both to

> **Music, and especially female performers, gave me a sense of freedom that was completely absent on our heavily censored government TV**

SPECIAL REPORT: UNSUNG HEROES

ABOVE: Iranian singer Golazin Ardestani wants to see the day when women can perform freely in Iran

perform without persecution, and to study for a master's in music psychology in London, Ardestani made a final attempt to plead her case and gain permission to record an album.

"I had to trick my way through the system just to get my foot in the door of the Department of Direction, where the man who granted permissions for male singers worked. But when I finally met him, he wouldn't even look at me, staring at the floor as he spoke," she said. She was told that Iran didn't need a Céline Dion.

Ardestani knew then there was no coming back. "Once I started singing freely, I would lose my home forever," she said. On the day she left, after Norouz (Persian New Year) in 2011, she decided she would dedicate everything to fighting for change.

"I promised myself that my music would carry the voices of those who can't be heard," she said. "There was no way for me to be fully myself as a musician, as a singer or even as a woman. They controlled every aspect of my voice, my body, my agency."

She knows that she cannot return, and is confident that if she did, she would be arrested and charged with *Mofsed fel-Arz*, or "spreading corruption on earth", due to her open challenges to what she calls Iran's "fabricated religious theocracy". This charge could carry a death sentence.

The songs she has finally had the freedom to create include *Haghame*, meaning "It's My Right", which is about the freedom to choose whether or not to wear the hijab. Another, *Khodavande Shoma*, translates to "Your God", and includes the lyrics: "Your god is sick, it seems – a sick, dangerous criminal. Your religious beliefs, death, and destruction. Your prayers are for murder and blood."

For female musicians in Iran, freedom is still out of reach. Many women rely on underground scenes, Ardestani told Index, but this comes with its own risks. Posting performances on social media can also lead to arrests, intimidation and the charge of *Mofsed fel-Arz*.

And censorship does not always respect borders. At a concert in Canada in 2023, designed to support the Woman, Life, Freedom movement, Ardestani was told she could not sing *Khodavande Shoma*, because the organisers believed it was "attacking people's religion". This, she said, is not what the song is about. Rather she is "confronting the twisted version of religion that the Islamic regime has created".

"I am an Iranian woman fighting for freedom and, specifically, for women's freedom of choice and speech. Yet here I was, outside of Iran, being told by an organiser – of a concert for freedom, no less – that I couldn't sing a song in a free country," she said.

She told the male Iranian organisers that she would sing that song, or not →

CREDIT: Laeticia Dumez

INDEXONCENSORSHIP.ORG **69**

sing at all. They relented.

For every performance Ardestani gives, another song in Iran is silenced. She often posts on social media about the plight of imprisoned Iranian musicians. She condemned the arrest of Zara Esmaeili, who often sang covers of international pop hits in public with her hair uncovered. One social media video showed Esmaeili performing Amy Winehouse's Back to Black. She was arrested on 25 July 2024, and it is believed that she has not been heard from since.

Ardestani is a huge admirer of Iranian rapper Toomaj Salehi, who won an Index Freedom of Expression Award in 2023. He was first arrested in 2022, and after being detained multiple times and tortured, he was charged with "corruption on earth", jailed and given the death sentence. The death sentence was dropped after campaigning from prominent musicians and human rights organisations including Index, and Salehi was released in early December.

"It's unimaginable that a musician, simply expressing himself through lyrics, could be sentenced to death for his art," Ardestani said. "Iranian music is powerful and resilient; it's the heartbeat of a people who have been silenced in many other ways. Each song is a form of resistance, a declaration of our existence and our hope."

As to why Salehi and other musicians are targeted, she has a strong theory: "They know the power of a good song, the potential of meaningful lyrics and the way music can unite people to inspire change."

For Ardestani now, everything is about fighting for freedom for all – not just in Iran, but globally. She describes music as a way to transform personal struggles into a collective moment. In another of her songs, *Betars Az Man*, or Fear Me, she sings:

"The butterfly is fleeing its cocoon.
Fear me, as I am that butterfly.
Fear me, as freedom is my voice."

In her upcoming song *Zaloo*, she says she will offer her vision for ending theocracy in Iran – a musical call to action. For Ardestani, music is a form of rebellion. And as she told Index, far from being afraid herself: "Those who wish to silence me should be the ones who are afraid." ✖

Katie Dancey-Downs is assistant editor at Index

> Iranian music is powerful and resilient; it's the heartbeat of a people who have been silenced in many other ways

BELOW: "Those who wish to silence me should be the ones who are afraid," says Ardestani

SPECIAL REPORT ◆ UNSUNG HEROES

In tune with change

From Fela Kuti to Burna Boy, Afrobeats has long been a symbol of resistance against brutality and corruption in Nigeria, writes **TILÉWA KAZEEM**

MUSIC HAS ALWAYS been more than just a mirror for Nigeria's effervescent spirit. It exists as a force that speaks truth to power and amplifies the voices of the oppressed, and musicians have long wielded their art to confront injustice and call for change.

Since its independence in 1960, the country's history has been marked by episodes of torrid leadership and political upheaval – a turbulent journey that led to its first military coup just six years after gaining independence.

Against this backdrop, musicians became activists, with the late Fela Kuti at the forefront, draping Nigeria's hypocrisies in rhythm and biting lyrics with anthems such as Zombie.

From Sound Sultan's *Jagbajantis* (Mathematics), which captures the struggle of Nigerians seeking greener pastures, to today's icons including Burna Boy and Falz, who use their platforms to rally for justice, Nigerian music has long been intertwined with social and political activism. Nigerians continue to confront the same struggles that Kuti sang about years ago.

At a time when issues such as police brutality, corruption and economic inequality weigh heavily on the nation, music has become a weapon – it is a tool that brings people together, challenges authority and ignites movements.

Historical background

This tradition of musical activism isn't new; Nigerian artists have long used their music to confront political and social issues. No one embodied this more than Kuti, the legendary pioneer of Afrobeats, whose songs continue to resonate as symbols of defiance.

In Zombie, he criticised the military's robotic obedience to corrupt leaders, using sharp, satirical lyrics and relentless beats to depict the oppressive reality faced by ordinary Nigerians.

For this, he endured raids, arrests and assaults – yet he never muted his message. Instead, these experiences became fuel for his pioneering music.

In Coffin for Head of State – written after his mother (who was herself a prominent women's rights activist) was thrown from a balcony, his sanctuary was desecrated and he was beaten by the military – he confronted how religion was used as a smokescreen while those in power fed off Nigeria's resources.

He sang: "Look Obasanjo! Before anything at all, him go dey shout: 'Oh Lord, oh Lord, oh Lord, Almighty Lord! Oh Lord, oh God!'"

In his view, these same leaders "do bad, bad, bad, bad, bad, bad things", using religion as a cover for their corrupt actions.

In Authority Stealing, he exposed how "authority people" steal without repercussions while petty thieves are swiftly arrested and jailed. Kuti sharply contrasted small-time criminals with those in power, singing: "Authority people them go dey steal, public contribute plenty money, na authority people dey steal."

His verses paint a vivid image of how authority figures commit theft on a grand scale, beyond the reach of traditional crime and punishment.

As he put it: "Armed robber him need gun, authority man him need pen… if gun steal eighty thousand naira, pen go steal two billion naira."

Kuti's lyrics underscored his belief that the true power – and danger – lay with those in authority, who wielded pens to drain public resources far beyond what any armed robber could ever steal.

Kuti's songs, raw and uncompromising, set a powerful precedent, proving that music could be a tool of resistance in the face of overwhelming power.

Inspired by his activism, other artists continued to push boundaries. Musicians such as Sonny Okosun, with songs including Which Way Nigeria?, →

CREDIT: Philippe Gras / Alamy

LEFT: Fela Kuti, who is widely regarded as the founding father of Afrobeats, performs at Hippodrome de Pantin in Paris on 15 March 1981

In a society where speaking out can bring real consequences, each beat and lyric becomes an act of courage

→ voiced opposition to apartheid and colonial legacies, linking Nigerian struggles to the broader African liberation movement.

These pioneers laid a foundation for later activism. Songs such as Eedris Abdulkareem's Jaga Jaga and Charly Boy's 1990 transformed Nigerian music into a weapon against oppression and created a lasting legacy.

Modern-day impact
Today, Nigerian artists continue this legacy, tackling new challenges that impact millions. During the #EndSARS protest movement against police brutality – which called for the disbandment of the Special Anti-Robbery Squad – musicians including Burna Boy and Falz emerged as powerful voices of the people.

Burna Boy's 20 10 20 was named after the date of the Lekki Toll Gate shooting, when 12 unarmed protesters were killed by the Nigerian Army. The song, haunting and direct, captures the trauma many Nigerians felt – a memory the government sought to silence.

In Monsters You Made, from his Grammy-winning album Twice As Tall, Burna Boy similarly confronts how greed in power has turned everyday citizens into "monsters".

Falz, an artist and lawyer, has been unwavering in his commitment to speak out against social injustice, corruption and Nigeria's poor state of affairs. His 2019 album, Moral Instruction, tackles these issues directly, even sampling Fela's Zombie in the track Follow Follow.

In This Is Nigeria, Falz blends hip-hop with social commentary to expose the country's deep-rooted issues, from corruption to religious extremism, capturing the ironies and struggles of everyday Nigerian life, sparking conversations nationwide.

With social media amplifying these messages, musicians now reach global audiences, fostering solidarity and greater awareness of their country's realities.

Music as a cultural connector and catalyst for change
But Nigerian music doesn't only highlight oppression – it also unites and empowers.

It has become a cultural connector, rallying communities within the country and across the diaspora. For young people especially, these songs resonate deeply, reflecting their lives and struggles and inspiring them to see themselves as agents of change. The music builds a collective identity, empowering the youth and giving them a sense of purpose.

International listeners have also connected with these narratives, with Nigerian artists sparking global conversations on social justice.

This was evident during #EndSARS, when Afrobeats icons Davido, Burna Boy, Falz and Wizkid joined rallies both in Nigeria and abroad. This visibility created a bridge, enabling cultural exchange and raising international awareness of Nigerian issues.

Challenges and limitations
Yet despite its power, musical activism in Nigeria faces significant challenges. Censorship looms constantly, with the authorities quick to silence dissenting voices. Musicians risk harassment, legal repercussions and even physical danger when they choose to speak out, making freedom of expression a fragile right. This presents a daunting barrier for artists who attempt to confront powerful institutions.

There's also the question of whether music alone can effect lasting change. While it certainly raises awareness, music

ABOVE: Afrobeats artist Burna Boy performs at State Farm Arena in July 2022 in Atlanta

often has its strongest impact when it complements larger movements, such as #EndSARS, when street protests and social media campaigns against police brutality amplified messages of resistance. This synergy gives a voice to the voiceless and strengthens the call for reform, suggesting that music's true power lies in its ability to inspire collective action.

However, since the Lekki Toll Gate shooting, Nigerians have become more cautious. Witnessing the government's ruthless response has deterred many from criticising them openly. The fear of being

SPECIAL REPORT: UNSUNG HEROES

met with violence simply for protesting has also made them less willing to risk peaceful demonstrations – leaving a culture of caution after that tragedy.

Despite these formidable challenges, Nigerian music remains an enduring testament to resilience and resistance. Musicians continue to echo the struggles of the people, using their voices to expose injustice and create space for dialogue. In a society where speaking out can bring real consequences, each beat and lyric becomes an act of courage – a defiant statement that change is possible.

As the world tunes in, Nigerian artists are no longer just voices of their nation – they have become ambassadors of truth on the global stage. Through the powerful language of music, they bring their nation's struggles into international conversations, inviting listeners everywhere to witness and engage.

This growing global solidarity suggests that while music alone may not bring about all the answers, it has the power to build bridges, spark movements and inspire hope.

In the end, Nigerian music is more than a call for change. It is a unifying force that reminds millions, both at home and abroad, that the fight for justice is far from over. ✖

> **While music alone may not bring about all the answers, it has the power to build bridges**

Tiléwa Kazeem is a Nigerian columnist covering cultural issues

SPECIAL REPORT ◆ UNSUNG HEROES

Singing for a revolution

BOBI WINE tells **DANSON KAHYANA** that he is still standing up to oppression in Uganda, both politically and musically

IN UGANDA, TO be an opposition politician is to be a marked man or woman. You can be taken out of action at any time.

This is one of the lessons that president Yoweri Museveni's most formidable challenger – the popstar-turned-politician Robert Kyagulanyi Ssentamu, popularly known as Bobi Wine – has learnt.

In September, just weeks before talking to Index, Wine was taken to hospital after the police fired tear gas to disperse his supporters in the town of Bulindo, about 17km north of Kampala. A canister exploded and fragments of the casing had to be removed from his leg.

Museveni, who stormed to power in January 1986 after waging a five-year guerrilla war against former President Milton Obote's regime, has done everything in his power to bring the democratic process in Uganda to a halt.

He has changed the constitution on two occasions. In 2005, he removed the term limits (which stipulated that nobody could serve as president beyond two five-year terms) and in 2017, he removed the age limit (which stipulated that nobody could stand for president if they were older than 75). He turned 80 this year, but these amendments have enabled him to stay in power almost as a monarch – a point that was made by Joshua B Rubongoya in his 2007 book, Regime Hegemony in Museveni's Uganda: Pax Musevenica.

Elections are held in Uganda, but they are usually a sham. Museveni is always assured of victory as he appoints the people who preside over elections. He ensures that the police not only intimidate voters but also brutalise opposition politicians, as myriad observers have noted.

The violence meted out to opposition politicians does not end with elections – it is more or less a daily happening.

In August 2018, Wine survived an assassination attempt when a security operative opened fire on his car, believing that Wine – and not his driver, Yasin Kawuma – was at the steering wheel. Nobody has been arrested for Kawuma's murder.

Beyond physical violence, Wine has also suffered as an artist through the government's ceaseless quest to silence him. There's effectively a ban on Wine's live music, as he was last allowed to hold a concert in November 2018. Even then, the police first blocked the show several times, setting several impossible conditions to frustrate him. Public venue owners were also intimidated into not hosting his shows.

"Before joining politics in 2017 as a member of parliament for Kyadondo County East constituency in Wakiso District, Central Region, I used to hold at least two major concerts every year – on Easter Sunday and on Boxing Day," Wine told Index.

"When we attempted to hold these concerts in 2019 and 2020, the military took over the venues. They claimed that I was using music concerts to pass political messages. Ironically, artists who are paid by the regime can hold concerts and pass any political messages as long as those messages are in support of the autocratic regime."

Wine and his team decided to hold the concerts at his own property, One Love Beach, in Busabala. They also sought redress through the courts, which declared the blockages illegal. But in an autocratic regime the law does not matter if it goes against the official party line, and the ruling was ignored.

"Basically, the regime in Uganda has criminalised my music," said Wine. "Many radio stations and TV stations hesitate to play our music for fear that the regime might clamp down on them."

He has been denied access to radio stations on numerous occasions – especially those outside Kampala, where the regime deliberately keeps people in the dark.

"Sometimes, I am plucked out of a radio station even after the programme has started, as happened in Hoima, a city in western Uganda," he said. "In fact, radio proprietors who have had the courage to host us have faced numerous challenges, including struggling to renew their licences."

Sarah Muhindo, managing director of Kasese Guide Radio, confirmed to Index that hosting opposition politicians came with a lot of pressure, including being summoned by the authorities for "guidance" on how questions asked of politicians should be "balanced" to avoid bias.

The message to the radio station managers and owners is clear: "We are watching what you are doing and we are

> While autocratic regimes use censorship to silence critical voices, sometimes it is that censorship that amplifies our voices

SPECIAL REPORT: UNSUNG HEROES

ABOVE: Musician-turned-politician Bobi Wine campaigns in Hoima, Uganda, in 2019

listening to what your visitors are saying."

However, Wine sees a ray of light even in the dark tunnel of dire circumstances in which he operates.

"With all the censorship and the clampdown on our political activities, many people around the world have picked-up interest in our music and made every effort to look for it online or from other sources," he said. "While autocratic regimes use censorship to silence critical voices, sometimes it is that censorship that amplifies our voices."

After Wine did so much to awaken artists as advocates for social justice issues on behalf of the masses, Museveni's brother Salim Saleh – chief co-ordinator of the government's Operation Wealth Creation (OWC) – compromised artists and music producers with money and other favours.

This included handpicked artists being given training workshops after the Covid-19 pandemic and cash bailouts, which the OWC denied were being offered. These actions were widely understood to have been a way of dissuading them from working with Wine.

Early this year, Museveni appointed a popular music promoter, Balaam Barugahara, as a minister. It was common knowledge that he had previously avoided working with musicians critical of the regime. In August, Museveni appointed another musician, Eddy Kenzo, as a senior presidential adviser.

Both appointments were widely considered to do two things: reward musicians and promoters who distanced themselves from Wine as a way of weakening him, and send a message that any musician or promoter who is critical of the government can "convert" and become pro-Museveni, reaping the rewards.

However, some artists such as Ssemanda Manisul (popularly known as King Saha) and Michael Kakande (also known as Kapalaga) have →

CREDIT: SOPA Images Limited / Alamy

INDEXONCENSORSHIP.ORG 75

RIGHT: Bobi Wine leaves a Kampala court in 2020, after he asked the judge to reconsider unconstitutional attempts by the Ugandan government to stop his political gatherings

→ continued to make a stand by releasing revolutionary songs. King Saha's shows have repeatedly been cancelled, while Kapalaga sings in exile.

Wine continues to sing, sometimes using allegories to disguise his message. Songs such as *Kyarenga* and *Nalumansi*, might sound like love songs on first hearing but are intentionally loaded with political messages about oppression, opportunism and liberation.

"You have to use imagery and proverbial language in order to elude censorship, and even possible prosecution," he said, pointing out that radio stations brave enough to play his songs are more comfortable playing those that have political meanings hidden behind love lyrics.

"For instance, I don't remember any radio station in Uganda playing Christopher Ssebaduka's *Ogenda*, which I redid in the aftermath of the rigged 2021 presidential election, because I was very direct in that song. Our song directed at security operatives, *Afande*, also faced extreme censorship as the mainstream media was ordered not to play it."

Wine has been able to use platforms such as YouTube, Facebook, Instagram and X to pass on his message. But the regime imposed a social media tax in 2018, forcing people to pay to use popular platforms to limit "gossip". This did not deter Ugandans from re-sharing Wine's songs. Museveni then banned Facebook in January 2021, ahead of the contentious election, accusing the company of arrogance after it removed a network of fake accounts and pages linked to his re-election campaign. The ban has not been lifted, although Ugandans continue to access the platform through VPNs.

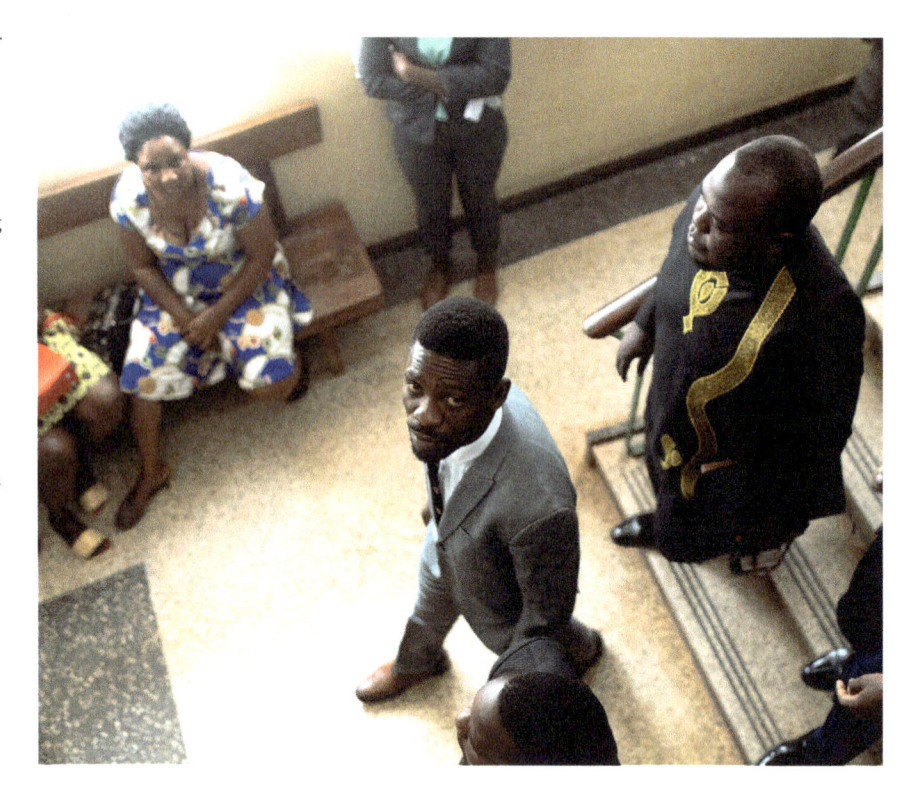

Wine is also collaborating with international artists to amplify his message across borders. He and co-singer Ali Bukeni, popularly known as Nubian Li, featured in a single entitled Such A Beautiful Day, released in August by the global World Funk Orchestra. The song celebrates hope and freedom in the quest for a better day – a message relevant to Ugandans. Seeing Wine and Li take part in the song without any police or military officials assaulting them is a reminder that a lot of work needs to be done to ensure that similar artistic freedom prevails at home.

Wine argues that there is nothing that people cannot achieve if they are united.

"This is why General Museveni is investing billions of shillings of taxpayers' money every year to ensure that artists do not unite. I wish my brothers and sisters would look beyond the small monies thrown at them and unite for the greater cause," he said.

He concluded by observing that autocrats throughout history have used censorship to try to silence musicians, authors and other creatives, but no amount of censorship ever prevented their inevitable fall.

He said: "I call upon Ugandans and all friends in the international community to do more to support all creatives in repressive regimes. By amplifying their voice and messages, you are playing your part in ensuring that eventual freedom is won." ✖

Danson Kahyana is a poet, author and scholar at Harvard Kennedy School, Stellenbosch University and Boston College. He is Index's contributing editor for East Africa

In an autocratic regime the law does not matter if it goes against the official party line

SPECIAL REPORT: UNSUNG HEROES

Cuba can't stop the music

COCO FUSCO tunes in to how musicians are hitting the wrong notes with those in power

PATRIA Y VIDA (Homeland and Life), the battle cry of the July 2021 mass protests in Cuba and the winner of two Latin Grammys, brought international attention to the political power of Cuban music.

A collaborative production by six Black Cuban musicians – Yotuel, Descemer Bueno, Alejandro Delgado and Randy Malcom of Gente de Zona in Miami, and El Funky and Maykel Osorbo in Havana – the song galvanised thousands of their compatriots to take to the streets in defiance of the government to demand freedom.

The song's success led to the imprisonment of Maykel Osorbo, and El Funky fleeing to the USA.

The July 2021 protests also resulted in the arrest of hundreds of Cubans, many of whom have received draconian sentences on trumped-up charges of sedition, sabotage and theft.

Maykel Osorbo is serving a nine-year sentence for allegedly resisting arrest, public disorder, violence against authorities and defamation of institutions, heroes and martyrs.

More than 1,000 Cuban political prisoners remain in prison. Of those, 10 are rappers and reggaetoneros – musicians involved in reggaeton, a style of music which blends dancehall, hip hop and Latin American music.

Maykel Osorbo, Dayán Gustavo Flores Brito, Ibrahim Domínguez Aguilar, Randy Arteaga Rivera, Wilmer Moreno Suárez, Juan Enrique Pérez Sánchez, Marcos Antonio Pintueles Marrero, Rolando Sardiñas and Yasmany González Valdés have all been behind bars since 2021. Marlon Hitachi Paz Bravo is detained but yet to be sentenced.

Dozens of musicians have left the country as repressive measures against cultural producers continue to escalate. In the last year, the government has revised its penal code to criminalise the use of social media to criticise the government and has also forbidden independent concert venues and music studios from registering as a MIPYME, the Cuban term for independently-run small businesses.

ABOVE: Promotional artwork for the release of Libertad, which focuses on the situation of Cuban artists who have been censored, imprisoned and forced into exile since the 2020 protests

Rappers Silvito el Libre (son of "revolutionary" troubadour Silvio Rodriguez), Los Aldeanos and Escuadron Patriota are among those who started their careers in Cuba but were compelled to relocate to the USA to avoid censorship. Musicians David D Omni and Kamankola are among the latest arrivals in Miami.

On 25 October, David Omni and Kamankola, together with El Funky and Doble 9, released a song entitled *Libertad* together with a music video by Luis Eligio D Omni, that lambasts the ➔

Dozens of musicians have left the country

→ Cuban government for its repression of the arts.

The song focuses on the situation of Cuban artists who have been censored, imprisoned and forced into exile since the November 2020 protest by Cuban artists at the Ministry of Culture.

They began protesting following an assault on the headquarters of the San Isidro Movement, an activist initiative spearheaded by currently imprisoned artist Luis Manuel Otero Alcántara, whose members include Maykel Osorbo, El Funky and formerly jailed rapper Denis Solis Gonzalez.

Repression of the arts has only grown since the later protests of July 2021.

The authors of *Libertad* underscore what they see as a contradiction between the oppressive conditions that Cuban artists face and the rosy image of Cuban culture presented by government-sponsored events such as the Havana Biennial, which takes place in Cuba every two years.

They seek to raise awareness of the island's political, economic and humanitarian crisis and continue to call for the liberation of Cuba's 1,063 political prisoners.

Attempts by the government to suppress rap and reggaeton are nothing new. Since the 1990s, these musical forms have evolved outside state channels and have long been vehicles for the expression of popular discontent.

Cuban rap music has been particularly attuned to the oppression of Black Cubans, whose standard of living has declined over the past three decades and who are far less likely to receive financial aid from family members abroad than others.

It should not be forgotten, however, that moves by the government to control the power, content and style of Cuban music extend back to the early days of the revolution.

In the early 1960s, musicians who refused to co-operate with the regime were forced into exile and their music was banned on the island – among them Celia Cruz, Olga Guillot, Meme Solis and Machito. La Lupe was also deemed unacceptable by revolutionary standards because of her wild vocal improvisations, so she relocated to New York in 1961.

In the 1960s and early 1970s, the government sought to wipe out "*Yanqui* (Yankee) Imperialist" influence by demonising rock music and classifying youths who listened to it as deviant. Magazines directed at young audiences featured cartoons that caricatured rock musicians and their fans.

In the 1980s, the rise of Miami-based Cuban-American musicians Gloria Estefan and Willy Chirino, both of whom have been openly critical of the Cuban government, led to their music being censored. Jazz saxophonist Paquito D'Rivera defected in 1980 and trumpeter Arturo Sandoval did the same in 1990 as both felt excessively

ABOVE: The cover of a 1965 edition of Revista Mella magazine features a cartoon depicting revolutionary militants stomping out the influence of the USA

LEFT: Cuban musicians are demanding "No More Dictatorship"

CREDIT: (above) Revista Mella; (left and right) Handouts

SPECIAL REPORT: UNSUNG HEROES

ABOVE: Cuban musicians El Funky, Kamankola, Doble 9 and David D Omni released Libertad at the end of October 2024

constrained by regulations.

Nueva Trova musician Pedro Luis Ferrer and the timba band La Charanga Habanera were censored in the 1990s due to their supposedly "counter-revolutionary" lyrics.

More recently, Gorki Aguila – leader of the punk rock band Porno Para Ricardo and author of several satirical songs that rail against Fidel Castro and Cuba's security apparatus – has served prison time as part of a sustained effort to silence the group. He went into exile in Mexico earlier this year.

> Repression of the arts has only grown since the protests of July 2021

Island-based musicians have been disproportionately affected by state repression for a number of reasons, while the income generated by state-sanctioned Cuban musicians' recordings and concerts abroad represents a significant benefit to a regime that is desperate for hard currency.

Music's political power has a lot to do with why it is targeted by the state. It is the artistic field that has the largest popular following, both in Cuba and abroad. Its potential impact as a vehicle for political messages is perceived by authorities as a threat to state control of public discourse and, ultimately, to government stability. Indeed, the success of Patria y Vida and its widespread appearance as graffiti throughout Cuba, its invocation by protesters and its frequent use by disgruntled citizens as a retort to police are clear indications of the capacity of music to mobilise anti-government sentiment.

It also signals a major shift with regard to the perception and reception of Cuban music globally.

For decades it has been the leftist lyrics of Nueva Trova singers such as Silvio Rodriguez that inspired progressive youths throughout the Spanish-speaking world and helped to create an image of Cuba as a tropical socialist paradise.

But after 60 years of championing the Cuban revolution, he now laments that "the current situation undermines any ideal convictions".

Even Silvio Rodriguez has changed his tune. ✖

Coco Fusco is an artist and writer based in New York. She is the author of Dangerous Moves: Performance and Politics in Cuba

'Brilliant'
Rana Mitter

'Vivid'
Wall Street Journal

'Remarkable'
Julia Lovell

'Passionate'
Kirkus Review

'Illuminating'
Yangyang Cheng

'Excellent'
New York Review of Books

'Recommended'
Ian Rankin

VIGIL
THE STRUGGLE FOR HONG KONG
JEFFREY WASSERSTROM
WITH AMY HAWKINS AND KRIS CHENG

'A great, snappy introduction to how Hong Kong got where it is today. Whereas many Sinologists focus on the exceptional qualities of Xi Jinping's China, Wasserstrom, a historian, looks at Hong Kong's troubles through a comparative lens. He reaches back into China's past, as well as looking around the world, to help the reader make sense of events in Hong Kong.'
Ben Bland, author and director of the Asia-Pacific programme at Chatham House

OUT 7 JANUARY 2025

buijones.com

COMMENT

"The business frequently turned a blind eye to mental illness. If the talent could turn up and deliver then it wasn't a problem"

MUSICIAN, HEAL THYSELF | MIKE SMITH | P.84

CREDIT: Gustavo Pantano / Alamy

Dangerous double standards

The closure of Al Jazeera's West Bank office is a symbol of Israel's repression of Palestinian journalists, writes **YOUMNA EL SAYED**

ABOVE: Palestinian artists in Gaza paint a mural for Al Jazeera journalist Shireen Abu Akleh, who was killed in 2022 while covering the storming of Jenin refugee camp in the West Bank

IN SEPTEMBER, ISRAELI soldiers raided the Al Jazeera office in Ramallah, in the occupied West Bank, and ordered the network's bureau to close for 45 days.

It was not the first media shutdown. In May, the army stormed the Al Jazeera bureau in East Jerusalem and closed it after confiscating its equipment, claiming that the network was a threat to national security.

Israel has also said that the network "incites terror" and "supports terrorist activities".

Israel has long exercised suppression of the freedom of the media in the occupied Palestinian territories. Many Palestinian journalists have been killed, attacked, threatened and arrested.

This has made their jobs in the occupied territories almost impossible. It's a constant life-threatening situation and Israel has deliberately targeted Al Jazeera journalists and their families on many occasions.

The killing of Palestinian-US journalist Shireen Abu Akleh in 2022; the targeting of many other colleagues' families in Gaza, including my own; the deliberate killing of Al Jazeera journalists in direct attacks – these are all crimes against press freedom and attempts to silence journalists.

Your press gear labels you as a direct target to the Israeli army, and the pain and worry of being a danger to your loved ones is indescribable.

Since October 2023, Israel's suppression of the press has stretched to foreign journalists, too,

> The pain and worry of being a danger to your loved ones is indescribable

Our job as journalists is to inform the public based on facts and evidence, not political agendas

as it has prevented all international journalists from exercising their right to cover one of the most brutal wars in recent history.

I believe this is an attempt to avoid exposure of crimes committed against the Palestinians and the crisis they face.

Al Jazeera has long been a prominent voice covering the Israeli-Palestinian conflict, and its presence in the region has been crucial for a global audience.

The network's coverage depends on a large number of journalists bringing together all aspects of the story at once.

Over the years, it has built a reputation for its commitment to telling the story from both sides of the divide, and many people around the world turn to Al Jazeera for the latest developments and breaking news stories.

Its coverage isn't just a reflection of events on the ground – it is an avenue for audiences, globally, to understand the complexities of these events. And the closure of its offices sends a chilling message.

For years, Al Jazeera has been criticised by Israeli officials for what they allege is biased reporting. But such accusations overlook the network's fundamental journalistic principle: to show the full spectrum of the story.

Al Jazeera's coverage is notably impartial. I say this because it brings to light the narratives of both Israelis and Palestinians, ensuring that no side goes unheard. Its reporters don't shy away from broadcasting the pain and suffering endured by civilians on either side of the conflict. Whether it's an Israeli family mourning after a rocket attack, Palestinians in Gaza grappling with the aftermath of airstrikes, or settler violence and illegal confiscation of Palestinian land in the West Bank, Al Jazeera's cameras capture the human realities.

All this is clear in its coverage since the beginning of the current war.

On 7 October 2023, my reporting as a Gaza correspondent was on the Palestinian attacks on Israeli towns. Other stories I worked on for my colleagues in Israel highlighted the aftermath of these attacks and the impact on Israeli families.

This objectivity is rare and invaluable in a conflict where misinformation, propaganda and one-sided narratives often dominate. Where many news outlets have taken up clear ideological stances, Al Jazeera has remained steadfast in its commitment to neutrality. It's not just about giving airtime to both sides – it's about letting the facts speak for themselves.

And this is the true objective of journalism in the first place. Our job as journalists is to inform the public based on facts and evidence, not political agendas.

To suggest that this impartiality is a threat worthy of office closures is to misconstrue the role of journalism in a so-called democratic society. The very essence of a free press is to inform the public, to provide transparency and to hold those in power accountable. Silencing a media outlet such as Al Jazeera is a direct assault on these values.

The closure of its offices also highlights a double standard. Israeli authorities have allowed other international news agencies to continue their operations, many of which cover the conflict in ways that are far less nuanced or balanced. Yet a network that works diligently to present both Israeli and Palestinian perspectives is being targeted and its journalists are constantly under attack.

What does this say about the future of press freedom in Israel and the occupied territories? ✘

Youmna El Sayed is a Gaza Strip correspondent at Al Jazeera English

53(04):82/83|DOI:10.1177/03064220241306633

RIGHT: The Al Jazeera English newsroom in Doha, Qatar

Musician, heal thyself

MIKE SMITH reflects on the epidemic of silence that has surrounded mental health in the music industry

THE RECENT PASSING of One Direction's Liam Payne made me reflect on my first encounter with him during the filming of The X Factor in the autumn of 2010.

The confident 17-year-old from Wolverhampton enthusiastically posed for pictures with my daughter before delivering a note-perfect performance on the show that night. There was no doubt in my mind that he had a golden career ahead of him.

In the spring of 2012, I found myself in a small, windowless room in the bowels of Cardiff City Football Club judging the first round of potential contestants for that year's competition.

During the day, I sat with an assistant producer on the show and ate a large jar of Haribo as we auditioned countless hopefuls. By the early evening, I never wanted to hear Rolling In the Deep again. A pain in my right shoulder had spread down my body and I felt like I was seizing up. When I saw the doctor the following day, she asked what my lifestyle was like. I explained that I had been to the USA twice that month, worked most evenings and drank coffee to power through the days.

"I can see it in your eyes," she told me. "They are dull, you have no energy, the fire in your soul is out." She prescribed immediate bed-rest and suggested I read The Presence Process by Michael Brown, a spiritual manual encouraging being present in the moment. I followed her advice, took some time off work and read the book. Four weeks later, I left my job running Columbia Records in the UK.

I had been working flat out in the music business for 25 years and was suffering from acute work-related stress, coming close to physical collapse. And yet I was incapable of doing anything about it until my body intervened on my behalf.

As the head of a record label, I hadn't recognised the symptoms of exhaustion and mental ill health in myself, and yet I was responsible for the wellbeing of both my staff and the artists on the roster.

My story was not uncommon in the music industry at the time. Whilst shows such as The X Factor had a duty of care to the contestants and employed a psychiatrist to help anyone with potential problems, the pressures on anyone following a career on the front line of popular music can very easily become too much to bear.

The business frequently turned a blind eye to mental illness. If the talent could turn up and deliver then it wasn't a problem.

Signing a record deal with a major label can feel like answered prayers. Everything an act has worked towards has brought them to this point and finally they can devote their lives to making music.

No matter how much you anticipate making it in the music business, however, nothing can prepare you for the impact of fame. As Blur's bass player Alex James put it recently: "Success will fuck you up far more than failure."

The demands on the time of a successful artist are huge, and they are often on the go from early morning until the middle of the night if they are performing live or working in the studio.

As a creative professional, they also carry the burden of relying upon their talent – which has got them this far – to take them to the next level. Their every move is being publicly scrutinised and any private life has evaporated. It is no surprise, then, that musicians frequently resort to stimulants to help them through the day, brimming with confidence, only to need something else to help them go to sleep. It is a potent and sometimes deadly cocktail.

The worst part is that you are supposed to be living the dream and any suggestion that your life is

ABOVE: The late Liam Payne with his former One Direction bandmate Zayn Malik in 2012

> **I had been working flat out in the music business for 25 years and was coming close to physical collapse**

For too long, the music industry ignored the pressures of work for artists and those behind the scenes

anything less than perfect feels like letting people down.

For too long, the music industry ignored the pressures of work for artists and those behind the scenes across the business.

By 2017, I was running a major music publishing company and had a much better understanding of mental health than I had five years earlier. I was shocked to discover that a substantial proportion of our songwriters were suffering with psychological problems which prevented them from working. The stress of being able to consistently deliver hit songs takes an enormous toll and many writers simply couldn't find a way forward.

From that point onwards, we made the decision to include in our songwriter contracts a provision to access professional mental health care. The staff at the company were taught about the importance of looking after their own wellbeing and they had access to full healthcare if it was needed. We formed close relationships with mental health charities such as Music Support.

The music business in 2024 is very different from the one I joined in the mid-eighties and it has made huge strides in the field of mental health over the past 10 years.

All the major music companies have professionals on the payroll, working with their staff and their artists. Particular attention is paid to young artists at the beginning of their careers as well as to those that are exiting the company and facing an uncertain future. There is a clear understanding of the need for personal time and breaks in the schedule to rest and recuperate. The brutal schedules of the past have been moderated.

I am optimistic for the future as the new generation of executives coming through have a much greater understanding of wellbeing than I did when I was younger.

As a result, the artists and musicians in their care are finding themselves in a much kinder and safer environment.

But sadly, it seems it was all too late for Liam Payne. ✖

Mike Smith has worked in the music business for more than 40 years. He is currently writing his memoirs

BELOW: People pay tribute to Liam Payne at St Peters Collegiate Church in his hometown of Wolverhampton

LEFT: Donald Trump and Victor Orban at the NATO Summit 2017 in Brussels, Belgium

Democracy, but not as we know it

Donald Trump's re-election is indicative of a broader global trend towards a new age of veiled authoritarianism, writes **MARTIN BRIGHT**

HYBRID REGIMES, ILLIBERAL democracies, democraships, democraturas: these are all slightly terrifying new terms for governments around the world which are drifting towards authoritarianism. We have been used to seeing the world through the binary geopolitics of the more-or-less democratic free world on one side and the straightforward dictatorship on the other. But what is Hungary under Viktor Orbán? Or Narendra Modi's India? And, as the world comes to terms with the reality of US president Donald Trump's second term, will the USA become a hybrid regime dominated by tech oligarchs and America First loyalists?

At a recent conference in Warsaw held by the Eurozine, a network of cultural and political publications, Tomáš Hučko, from the Bratislava-based magazine Kapitál Noviny, told the dispiriting story of his country's slide towards populist authoritarianism. The Slovak National Party, led by the ultranationalist prime minister Robert Fico, drove a coach and horses through media and cultural institutions, he explained, beginning with the Culture Ministry itself. Fico then changed the law to take control of public radio and TV. The heads of the Slovak Fund for the Promotion of the Arts, the National Theatre, the National Gallery and the National Library were fired and replaced with party loyalists, and a "culture strike" was met with further attacks on activists and government critics.

"There were constant attacks on the journalists by the prime minister, including suing several writers," said Hučko.

Fellow panellist Mustafa Ünlü, from the Platform 24 media group in Turkey, spoke of a similar pattern in his country, where president Recep Tayyip Erdoğan's government has withdrawn licences from many independent broadcasters.

It is tempting to suggest that these illiberal democracies are a passing political trend. But the problem, according to several Eurozine delegates, was that such regimes have a tendency to hollow out the institutions and leave them with scars so deep that they are difficult to heal.

Agnieszka Wiśniewska, from Krytyka Polityczna, a network of Polish intellectuals, sounded a note of extreme caution from her country's eight years of rule under the Catholic-aligned ultra-right Law and Justice Party. Although the party was beaten by prime minister Donald Tusk's centrist Civic Coalition in last year's elections, the damage to democracy has been done. "There is the possibility of reversing the decline," she said. "But the state media was turned into propaganda media."

In part, she blamed the complacency of politicians such as Tusk himself. "Liberals didn't care enough," she said.

Writing on contemporary hybrid regimes in New Eastern Europe, an English-language magazine which is part of the Eurozine network, Italian political scientist Leonardo Morlino identifies a key moment in July 2014 when Hungarian leader Viktor Orbán began using the expression "illiberal democracy".

He later clarified what he meant by this: that Christian values and the Hungarian nation should take precedence over traditional liberal concerns for individual rights. For Morlino, however, Hungary is not the only model of a hybrid regime. He provides a list of countries in Latin America (Bolivia, Colombia, the Dominican Republic, Ecuador, Guatemala, Haiti, Honduras, Mexico and Paraguay) with "active, territorially widespread criminal organisations, high levels of corruption and the inadequate development of effective public institutions" where democracy is seriously weakened. Meanwhile, in eastern and central Europe he recognises that Russian influence has created the conditions for hybrid regimes in Armenia, Georgia, Moldova and even Ukraine.

The term "democratura" comes from the French "démocrature" and combines the concepts of democracy and dictatorship. In English this is sometimes translated as "Potemkin democracy", which in turn comes from the phrase "Potemkin village", meaning an impressive facade used to hide an undesirable reality. This is named after Catherine the Great's lover Grigory Potemkin, who built fake show villages along the route taken by the Russian Empress as she travelled across the country.

It is tempting to suggest Trump is about to usher in an American Democratura, but none of these concepts map neatly onto the likely political context post-2025. The USA cannot be easily compared to the fragile democracies of the former Soviet Union, nor is it equivalent to the corrupt hybrid regimes of Latin America. It is true that Trump's former adviser Steve Bannon liked to talk about "illiberal democracy", but more as a provocation than a programme for government.

And yet there is an anti-democratic tone to the language used by Trump's supporters. In the BBC Radio 4 series on US conspiratorial ideology, The Coming Storm, reporter Gabriel Gatehouse noticed the increasing prevalence of the right-wing proposition that the USA is a "constitutional republic", not a democracy.

This line of thinking can be traced back to American ultra-individualist thinker Dan Smoot, whose influential 1966 broadcast on the subject can be found on YouTube. Smoot was an FBI agent and a fierce anti-communist who believed a liberal elite was running the USA, as he explained in his 1962 book The Invisible Government, which "exposed" the allegedly socialist Council on Foreign Relations.

Such rhetoric is familiar from the recent election campaign, which saw Trump attacking Kamala Harris as a secret socialist and pledging to take revenge on the "deep state".

There are worrying signs that Republicans under Trump will be working from an authoritarian playbook, and this could have a chilling effect on the media. Last month, the Republican-controlled US House passed a bill that, if signed into law, would give the government powers to target and punish non-profits it deems to support "terrorism". Critics argue such a law could be abused by Trump to unfairly target his political opponents. Similar laws have already been passed in Modi's India and Putin's Russia.

Trump has consistently attacked critical media as purveyors of "fake news". He has suggested that NBC News should be investigated for treason and that ABC News and CBS News should have their broadcast licences taken away. He has also said he would bring the independent regulator, the Federal Communications Commission, under direct presidential control. In one of his more bizarre statements, he said he wouldn't mind an assassin shooting through the "fake news" while making an attempt on his life.

Whether a Trump administration emboldened by the scale of the Republican victory will seriously embark on a project to dismantle American democracy is yet to be seen. The signs that the president has authoritarian proclivities are clear and he has made his intentions towards the mainstream media explicit.

Hybrid democracy may not quite be the correct terminology here. We may need a whole new lexicon to describe what is about to happen. ✖

Martin Bright is editor at large at Index

53(04):86/87|DOI:10.1177/03064220241306636

> There are worrying signs that Republicans under Trump will be working from an authoritarian playbook

ABOVE: Narendra Modi, Prime Minister of India, celebrating his party's victory in the Maharashtra Assembly elections and in several bypolls at BJP headquarters in November 2024

GLOBAL VIEW

Silence has to be permitted in a world with free speech

Index CEO **JEMIMAH STEINFELD** reflects on the growing pressure to take a political stance or be damned

I'M A VERBOSE person, but I could write a paean for silence. It is something many of us need baked into our day. It is a right granted to those who are being questioned by police; concerts start with the audience being told to hush; Quakers worship almost entirely in it. Silence is profoundly valuable on a personal, political and legal level.

At times it conveys a great deal on its own. In China in 2022, demonstrators silently held up blank sheets of paper in protest at repressive Covid policies, a clever tactic used to evade repercussions. Other times it means little to nothing at all.

But in our increasingly connected lives, I fear we are losing respect for it.

"Your silence speaks volumes." This phrase, and iterations of it, have recurred frequently for me this past year. It started within days of 7 October 2023. Following the Hamas massacres across southern Israel, my Instagram newsfeed was full of posts from people saying that if those in their network didn't speak up in solidarity with the slaughtered Israelis, they were somehow complicit. Or didn't care about dead Jews. Or both.

Like most people I was profoundly shocked by 7 October, but I didn't post anything on Instagram. This was a personal decision down to how I interact with the platform. Instagram is my refuge, a place to distract myself from the dark world I work in through pictures of my friends' kids, holiday snaps and puppies. X, by contrast, is my political and professional space.

It's raw, unfiltered, often angry and, at least until recently, very useful for sourcing news. That divide works for me. Many use the platforms differently and I respect that.

Such respect, however, was not being offered by others on my feed. At the time, I spoke to a close friend about mutual connections who were posting these confrontational messages (we'd all visited Israel together as teens). The friend said they were careful about what they posted because of where they worked. I spoke to another friend, also connected to the region, who also was not posting – they said they were simply too shocked and that words were failing them. We were keeping quiet for a variety of reasons – none of which suggested indifference – but we were all feeling under pressure to say something at an already challenging time.

Months later, following Israel's brutal retaliation, my Instagram feed was filled with graphic images of Gazan children buried under rubble, juxtaposed with artificially generated memes such as "All Eyes on Rafah". That same line cropped up: "Your silence speaks volumes." There it was again: the judgement, the assumptions.

Of all the pressuring tools used on social media, shame is perhaps the most frequently employed. Weaponising this emotion didn't start with the war in Israel and Palestine – similar lines were uttered during the #MeToo and Black Lives Matter movements.

"A refusal to post is, at its core, a refusal to give up comfort. A refusal to give up your power as a privileged individual. Think about the real reasons you don't want to publish your support. There should be no valid excuse," wrote one blogger in a post that went viral during the "black square" trend following the murder of George Floyd in the USA.

At a basic level, I understand where the pressure comes from. People feel powerless today. They don't understand why politicians aren't listening to them. They want strength in numbers and for momentum to build by everyone taking a stand.

But even if the cause is important and the intention noble, forcing solidarity to garner support is problematic. No one should be castigated for not commenting on an issue, unless that issue is quite obviously in their lane – for example, if they are a politician. Respecting people's silence is as important as respecting people's speech.

It doesn't stop at shame. People are being punished for their lack of words. This is not as much, I should add, as those who have been punished for their speech connected to Israel

A dictatorship works on both censoring "wrong speak" and enforcing "right"

ABOVE: Protesters with blank sheets of paper gather in Sydney, Australia in 2022 in solidarity with a protest movement in China, following a deadly high-rise building fire in Urumqi

and Palestine, which is something I have frequently called out and will continue to do so. But it is enough for it to be a concern.

Consider two examples. Earlier this year, Index interviewed a Russian artist who had moved to Israel following the invasion of Ukraine. She had posted about 7 October but not on what had happened in Gaza afterwards. Her London exhibition on Vladimir Putin was cancelled because of this.

Then, this October, some 1,000 people in the book publishing world signed a statement calling for a boycott of Israeli cultural figures and organisations that they believed were complicit in genocide. The statement said institutions that "have remained silent observers of the overwhelming oppression of Palestinians" would be boycotted.

The assumption in these is that silence implies agreement with what is happening in the Palestinian territories. Of course, it could mean someone supports atrocities in Gaza. Equally it could mean they don't, with myriad reasons why they might not feel comfortable speaking on the public record. In the case of Israeli cultural institutions specifically, it's worth remembering that in the hybrid democratic state of Israel, people are being punished for speech against the war or in solidarity with Palestinians.

Just as we admire those who speak out – and campaign to protect their right to do so – we need to stop our attack on those who refrain. This is important for the reasons above and it's important because compelled speech is a mechanism of a dictatorship. Autocrats force people to sing national anthems, confess to crimes they didn't commit, cry in public when their leaders die and chant phrases that reinforce a state line. A dictatorship works on both censoring "wrong speak" and enforcing "right". We shouldn't adopt autocratic tools as a means to promote human rights.

Sometimes silence genuinely is wrong and should be highlighted as such – for example, a foreign minister of a democratic nation should rightly campaign for human rights to be upheld globally. But at other times, silence is understandable. It can be a form of protection, indicate contemplation or be a stopgap before we find words that work.

Respect for restraint, for silence, is a fundamental right, albeit a harder one to champion in this age of anger, frustration and hate. ✖

Jemimah Steinfeld is CEO at Index

Big Tech shouldn't punish women for seeking abortions

In the run-up to Trump 2.0, state and local governments must push tech companies to protect women's private data, says **RAINA LIPSITZ**

BIG TECHNOLOGY COMPANIES have enormous and outsized power. They control what information we can share and how, and demonstrate little transparency or accountability to users about what they are doing. They are too often permitted to set their own arbitrary standards, governing what we can and can't say on social media, and how and to whom these ever-shifting rules apply.

In no area is this more evident than in the battle between those who want to seek out and criminalise women for having an abortion and those who want to protect women's right to choose.

In recent years, technology has dramatically altered the abortion landscape for women in the USA. It is now possible to order safe and effective abortion pills online and find accurate information about how to use those pills. This represents an unprecedented and world-changing expansion of women's privacy and freedom. Thanks to improved access to medication, far fewer women will die or be traumatised, despite the US Supreme Court's 2022 decision to strip the country's women of federally guaranteed abortion rights.

But women's new-found abortion freedoms are under threat from powerful people who oppose privacy, freedom and safety for women, and corporatists who put business interests above human rights. With President Donald Trump's re-election things may be about to become a whole lot worse.

In March 2024, eight months before the election, I attended Visions for a Digital Future: Combating Online Suppression of Abortion Information, a panel discussion hosted by a coalition of rights and safe abortion access organisations including Amnesty International USA, Plan C, the Universal Access Project and Women on Web, along with experts from Le Centre ODAS and Fòs Feminista.

The panellists warned that tech companies were already suppressing information about reproductive health, either deliberately and as a matter of policy, or accidentally, such as when posts containing legitimate medical information trigger filters meant to block other kinds of content. Remedies have been piecemeal. Some organisations have been able to get accounts reinstated after meeting with contacts at Meta, but there is no democratic and transparent way of determining who gets access to vital medical information.

In one very recent case, Meta temporarily shut down the advertising account of Plan C, a group that provides up-to-date information on how US residents access abortion pills online, days before the US election, over claims of "inauthentic behaviour".

European lawmakers have already taken steps to bring Big Tech companies to heel. They have done so via laws like the EU's Digital Markets Act, a 2022 law which, among other things, requires large tech companies to get users' consent before tracking them for advertising purposes; and the European Media Freedom Act (EMFA), which went into effect earlier this year, preventing large online platforms such as Facebook, X and Instagram from arbitrarily restricting or deleting independent media content.

Despite growing pressure from large parts of civil society, the USA has yet to pass federal legislation to meaningfully regulate Big Tech. Under a Trump presidency, the federal government is likely to go one step further and ask tech companies to use the data they hold to assist state and local law enforcement in tracking, prosecuting and jailing women for seeking abortions.

Some of the president-elect's most prominent supporters are anti-feminist tech executives like Elon Musk, the richest man in the world and an ardent foe of government regulation (of corporations); venture capitalist Peter Thiel, who has questioned the wisdom of ever allowing women to vote; and Blake Masters, failed congressional candidate and chief operations officer of Thiel Capital (Thiel's venture capital investment firm). All three have either previously expressed personal support for at least some level of abortion restriction

> It seems likelier that he'll take his cues from an oligarch like Musk than from his own vice president

COMMENT

ABOVE: Incoming president Donald Trump and tech billionaire Elon Musk will have immense control over what information women can access about abortion care

or given large sums of money to politicians committed to restricting it.

Knowing it was a liability for him, Trump made confusing and contradictory statements about abortion on the campaign trail: once pro-choice, he bragged about having appointed the Supreme Court justices who overturned Roe v Wade.

By contrast, Vice President-elect JD Vance is an open theocrat who has pressured federal regulators to rescind a Biden administration rule that prevents police from accessing the private medical records of women who cross state lines to get reproductive health care, according to investigative news outlet The Lever.

Project 2025, the 900-plus-page handbook assembled by the right-wing Heritage Foundation and drafted in part by dozens of former Trump administration officials, indicates that a second Trump administration will seek to increase federal surveillance of pregnant people nationwide. They will most likely do this partly by requiring states to report abortion data and cutting federal funding to those that don't comply. That data could put women and health care providers in serious danger of prosecution and/or jail time. State law enforcement officials could pressure or compel tech companies to collect and share it.

This has already happened in the USA under a Democratic administration. Facebook's 2022 decision to comply with a Nebraska police officer's request for private data enabled the state to try, as an adult, a 17-year-old girl facing criminal charges for ending a pregnancy. Facebook handed over private messages the girl and her mother had exchanged in which the two discussed obtaining abortion pills, according to The Guardian.

The extent of the data Facebook handed over is unclear, but it's apparent that companies like Facebook's parent company Meta →

Many of the largest tech companies in the world have refused to clarify how they will handle law enforcement requests for abortion-related data

CREDIT: AP Photo / Alex Brandon / Alamy

INDEXONCENSORSHIP.ORG **91**

LEFT: Women's rights advocates protesting the closure of an Iowa Planned Parenthood clinic in 2017. Under Trump's government, more closures could be imminent

→ cannot be trusted to safeguard users' privacy. Many of the largest tech companies in the world have refused to clarify how they will handle law enforcement requests for abortion-related data. While Meta does not allow users to gift or sell pharmaceuticals on its platform, it does, in theory, allow them to share information about how to access abortion pills, although enforcement of that policy has been inconsistent and non-transparent.

One ray of hope is that there's a small chance that Trump will retain Lina Khan, Biden's pick for chair of the US Federal Trade Commission (FTC). Khan has advocated for restraining the tech industry's power and is seen as a threat. Days before the election, Musk wrote on X that Khan "will be fired soon." Yet Vance has defended Khan, saying in a recent television interview that "she's been very smart about trying to go after some of these big tech companies that monopolise what we're allowed to say in our own country."

Best known as an anti-monopolist, Khan has brought lawsuits against data brokers trafficking in geolocation data, a crucial bulwark against efforts by anti-abortion prosecutors to obtain women's private medical data. This is important because in 2023, 19 Republican attorneys general in states that criminalised abortion demanded access to women's private medical records in order to determine whether they had travelled out of state for care.

Under Khan, the FTC also cracked down on companies that extracted and misused customers' private data. Browsing and location data of the kind these companies were gathering can provide intimate details of a person's life, from their religious and political affiliations and sexual proclivities to their private medical decisions. Companies, knowing that most people would object to having this kind of data collected and shared, often hide what they are doing or mislead users about the extent of it.

It's not yet clear what Trump's top priorities will be as president, or who will have his ear. On the question of Khan, it seems likelier that he'll take his cues from an oligarch like Musk than from his own vice president. As Politico recently noted Vance will have "little agenda-setting power of his own" in the new administration.

Occasional anti-Big Tech rhetoric notwithstanding, neither Trump nor Vance cares about protecting women's privacy. If Khan is fired, it's extremely unlikely that any member of the Trump administration will take measures to safeguard medical data. State and local authorities will have to do everything in their power to pressure or require these companies to clarify why they are suppressing abortion-related content, and push them to fight requests that violate users' privacy in court.

Authorities should also push or force tech companies to take measures – such as not collecting certain data in the first place or making it more secure – that would make it difficult or impossible to comply with law enforcement requests designed to punish women for exercising a right recognised by most Americans and international law. Failure to do so will jeopardise women's lives, health and freedom. ✖

Raina Lipsitz is the author of The Rise of a New Left: How Young Radicals Are Shaping the Future of American Politics. Her work has appeared in The Appeal, The Atlantic, The Nation and The New Republic, among other publications

The extent of the data Facebook handed over is unclear

CULTURE

"We are acting as censors ourselves because
our approach is not to send anything
that can harm the prisoner"

CELL DREAMS: RUSSIA'S PRISONER ART | PETR PETRENKO | P.94

Cell dreams: Russia's prisoner art

MARK STIMPSON speaks with lawyer **PETR PETRENKO**, an exiled supporter of jailed Russian anti-war protesters

FOR SEVERAL YEARS now, Russian exiles have been writing letters back home to people jailed for opposing the war in Ukraine. These exiles have now been joined by many others worldwide and the number of political prisoners in Russia has topped 1,000.

Sometimes those prisoners send letters back, but they often send artworks as well.

The lawyer Petr Petrenko is one of those in exile who writes regularly. Petrenko grew up in St Petersburg and worked as a lawyer and university lecturer, moving to London in 2017 to study human rights law at Queen Mary University of London.

"I'm slowly pursuing my PhD, but mostly focused on anti-war activities because the full-scale invasion changed many things for many people and I'm one of those people," Petrenko told Index.

Petrenko began campaigning against the war in 2022 and now cannot return to his homeland.

He participates in letter-writing evenings in London, but similar events also take place in many cities around the world including in Montreal, Vienna and Yerevan.

He says many of the people who attend the events have some connection to Russia.

"Maybe they were born there, maybe they speak Russian," he said, "but we are interested in reaching out to the audiences in the cities where we live and we're trying to accommodate non-Russian speakers as well. So, for example when we hold letter-writing workshops we translate letters written in

CULTURE

> As well as letters, prisoners are also allowed to draw or paint art on their forms

English and when we receive replies, we translate them back."

Unlike in the early days of Index, letters from political prisoners do not need to be smuggled out as *samizdat* – a discreet practice of circulating censored literature in the former Soviet Union.

"There are several online platforms which allow you to upload your message and even photographs and then it goes to the facility where the person you are writing to is based. The authorities review this message because everything is subject to censorship and then they pass it on to the person," said Petrenko.

The rules around censorship vary by prison and in some you can even mention the war in Ukraine rather than having to refer to it as a 'special military operation'.

"You only know about it when you are trying to use certain words or discuss certain topics. We act as helpers in the process of letter-writing. We look at every letter written in our workshops from the perspective of whether it will pass the censorship, and if there are certain questionable things we slightly edit them. We are acting as censors ourselves in a way because our approach is not to send anything which can →

ABOVE AND OPPOSITE: Artist Anastasia Gennadyevna Dyudyaeva was sentenced to three years and six months in a penal colony for what authorities dubbed "a public call for terrorism".

The courts said that Dyudyaeva had placed postcards with poems in Ukrainian "calling for reprisals against Russian President Vladimir Putin" in a supermarket in St Petersburg.

Her art features another anti-war protester who was jailed for his opposition to the Putin government: the pianist, writer and activist Pavel Mikhailovich Kushnir.

Kushnir was born in 1984 in Tambov and was identified as an exceptional talent from an early age, performing the complete cycle of 24 Preludes and Fugues by Dmitri Shostakovich at the age of 17. He graduated from the Moscow Conservatory in 2007 and was invited to become a soloist for Birobidzhan Regional Philharmonic in 2023.

Kushnir was a civil activist throughout his career but in 2024 was accused of making public calls for terrorist activity after publishing a video on YouTube which called the Bucha massacre "a disgrace to our homeland" and labelled Putin as a fascist.

Kushnir was detained in custody in May 2024. On 27 July, he died in the Birobidzhan pretrial detention centre following a hunger strike.

Anastasia Dyudyaeva produced the art as a tribute after his death.

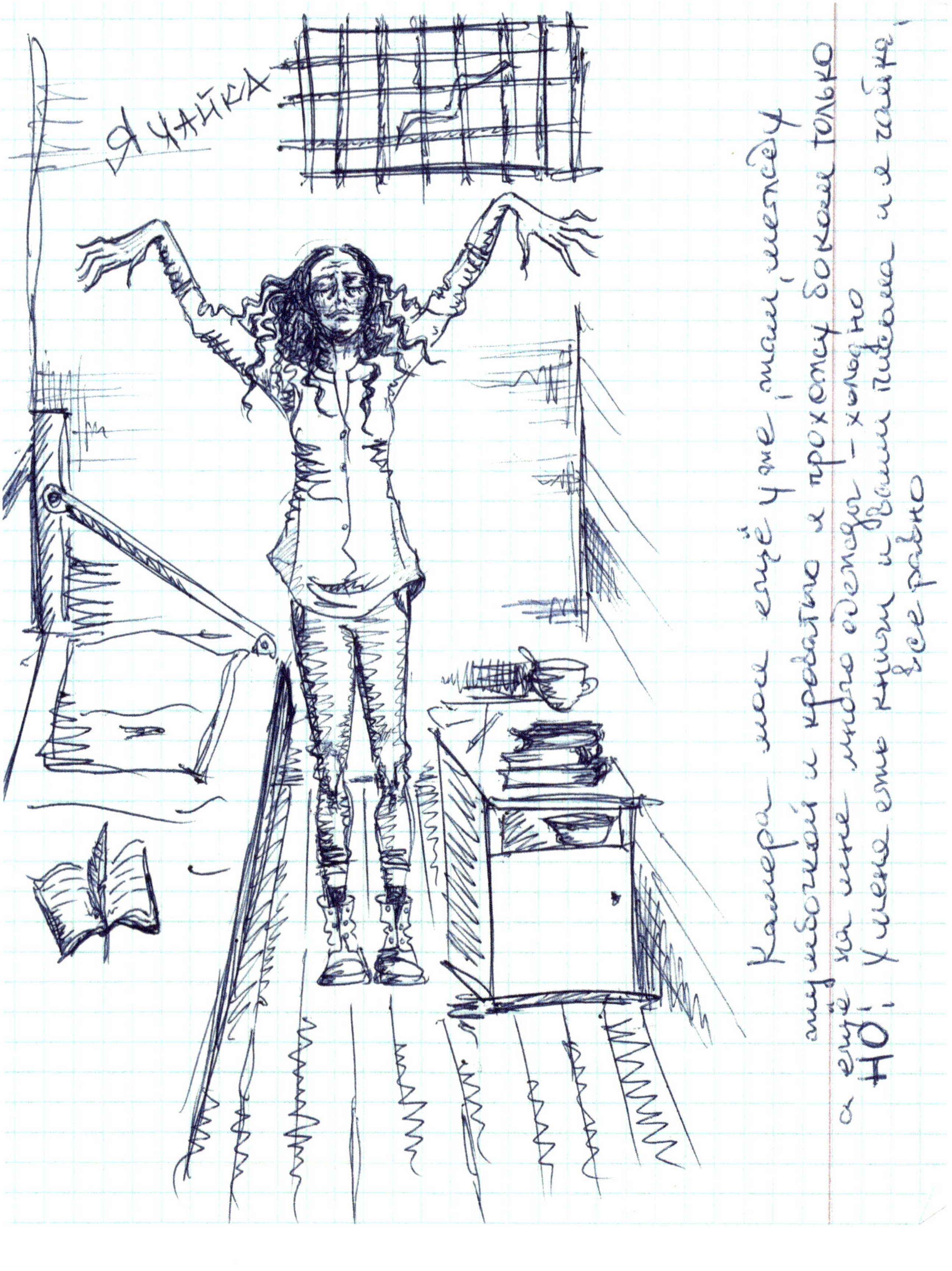
Я ЧАЙКА
а ещё на мне много одежды – холодно
всё равно

OPPOSITE: Lyudmila Aleksandrovna Razumova was sentenced to seven years in prison for opposing Russia's invasion of Ukraine. She was born in 1967 and lived in the Tver Region before being detained in April 2022.

Razumova and her husband posted videos on social media about the actions of Russian armed forces in Ukraine. They also painted graffiti on buildings and other structures in towns and villages in the Tver region. According to media reports, Razumova was held in solitary confinement for nine months.

ABOVE: Daniil Vladimirovich Klyuka is a 28-year-old art teacher from the Lipetsk region. He has been sentenced to 20 years in prison for allegedly "financing a terrorist organisation" (sending money to his brother in Ukraine) and "high treason".

Petrenko said: "Daniil drew a place in Italy from where he received a letter and where his supporter is based and it is a way of kind of connecting. He imagines this place when he communicates with this person and we all hope to meet one day there or in any other free place without risks of repression."

harm the prisoner," said Petrenko.

Prisoners can reply to the messages, often from unknown correspondents.

As well as letters, prisoners are also allowed to draw or paint art on their forms which, unless they are censored, are sent back through the same online system.

To explain why writing letters to political prisoners is so important, Petrenko cites Maria Ponomarenko, currently imprisoned for anti-war posts: "Your letters inspire us, give us strength and confidence that there will be a dawn and the changes are inevitable. Your letters serve as a support – solid ground beneath our feet. Your letters are uplifting and help distract us from the unpleasant realities of the Russian penitentiary system." ✖

The artworks here were received from Anastasia Gennadyevna Dyudyaeva,

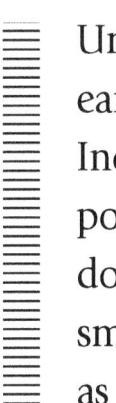

> Unlike in the early days of Index, letters from political prisoners do not need to be smuggled out as samizdat

Lyudmila Aleksandrovna Razumova and Daniil Vladimirovich Klyuka. You may write to Russia's political prisoners via https://letters-now.org/

Mark Stimpson is associate editor at Index

"You read literature to have a good time. Or why else would people go on doing it?" – Martin Amis

Sort your books out!

Reading doesn't have to be a solemn duty. But it can still be a challenge finding the right book sometimes. *Strong Words* comes out six times a year to make navigating the torrent of new stuff a pleasure. To subscribe, try a special Index on Censorship rate of just £3.75 a month, using the code INDEX24.

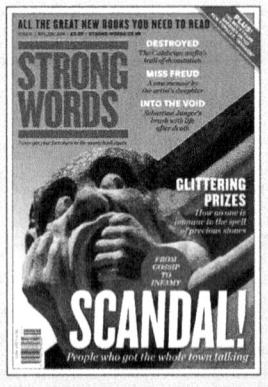

"Strong Words is absolutely brilliant. It's about books, all types of books, but it is written in such a fun and lively and jolly style." – Marina Hyde

Subscribe at: www.webscribe.co.uk/magazine/strongwords
Or call now on: 01442 820580
Never get your face stuck in the wrong book again
Offer only available to UK subscribers. Overseas rates available.

No catcher in the rye

STEPHEN KOMARNYCKYJ introduces and translates an excerpt from a novel by late Ukrainian writer and revolutionary, **HRYHORII KOSYNKA**, who was executed by the Soviets 90 years ago

NOBODY WHO SAW Hryhorii Kosynka read publicly in Kyiv in the 1920s ever forgot him. A young man with a blond thatch and simple face walked onto the stage and, with no notes or book, spoke his stories to an audience. They listened, mesmerised, while fellow writers speculated that a demon sat within him.

He had fought in the ranks of the socialist revolutionary Cossack Otaman Zelenyy's army during the Ukrainian War of Independence and had been in contact with Ukraine's first prime minister in exile. But the Soviet state, which in the 1920s let Ukrainians write in their own language to secure their loyalty, was watching. Kosynka was arrested on fake terrorist charges and executed aged 35 on 15 December 1934.

He was a member of the Executed Renaissance, a generation of Ukrainian language poets, writers and artists murdered or dispatched to labour camps by the Soviet regime in the 1920s and 1930s. The destruction of Ukrainian literature was accompanied by an artificial famine, the Holodomor, in which 3.9 million Ukrainians died. Kosynka would be erased from literature until Nikita Khrushchev took over as Russia's leader in 1953 and initiated the so-called "Khruschev thaw", when Soviet repression and censorship were relaxed. →

ABOVE: Part of the Ukrainian steppe where Hryhorii Kosynka's In The Rye is set. INSET: The Ukrainian writer Hryhorii Kosynka

> They listened, mesmerised, while fellow writers speculated that a demon sat within him

→ Reading Kosynka again, one is catapulted into a revolutionary Ukraine where there was the promise of a new world. Ukrainians then fought under different flags, and rather than depict social classes, Kosynka shows individuals in this period, and their fears and joys. He uses prose like an impressionist painter's brush and these texts are meant to be read like a painting where swatches of colour merge into half-recognisable shapes.

In The Rye (1925), a first-person account of a deserter from the Red Army running through the rye but with no catcher to save him, is set before the Red Army had fully conquered Ukraine. The vast plains of the Ukrainian Steppe grasslands, where the story is situated, were the home of the Cossacks, warriors whose role in founding a proto-Ukrainian state, the Zaporozhian Sich, is part of national mythology. Kornyi Dizik – whose surname is a derogatory term for a deserter – meets an old girlfriend who married a landowner for security, but who, too, is adrift in a chaotic, invaded country. The fragmentary style of Kosynka's writing, his sympathy with ideologically imperfect characters, and his use of the Ukrainian language all made him particularly subversive to the Soviets. Exactly 90 years after his death, the voice of this author speaks to our own time.

Stephen Komarnyckyj is a British-Ukrainian award-winning poet and literary translator

In The Rye

IT WAS ALL simple down to the smallest details: me, drowsy morning and grey steppe. I only remember dawn clearly, tearful with dew and the slightly bashful sun, bathing dimly in rye stalks.

"Well. Well… time to come out for a kiss."

I addressed the sun because it unceremoniously toyed with the hairs on my leg, lovingly inspected the tear in my trousers and laughed at me with bees' wings: "Dizik Dizik Dizik?"

This riled me because what does *dizik* mean? The word is terrifying because it reminds me of reality in two senses. Firstly, because in our revolutionary terminology, it means deserter; and secondly, I am one, comrade.

So there you are: when, I thought, the sun begins seeking deserters I won't go to the village, it's dangerous (this is customary with absconders) the levadas too, luckily it's Sunday, I'll sleep in the rye.

So I decided that, although the *levadas* allured me treacherously with willows and gardens smelling of wormwood and mint, my faithful comrade was the rye.

I lay in the valley where the Hordyna burial mound smoulders in the sun and before me lies the pillared track to Hnylyshche, Chornoslyvka, and further….

In the rye!

It was beautiful, ripening, and in a week or two it would be haystacks, but now it grew upwards: in my mind, scythes and sickles chimed and heavy ears of grain bent to earth but then an old stork walked solemnly through grass to the bog, bowed in all four directions, caught an

> But I remembered that, when a soldier saw a green shirt in the village, they aimed carefully, as at a dead willow, and yelled, shooting in fear, "Stop, you are not from here!"

unwary frog and with a dull clatter startled the wild duck on the water.

"That was a stupid frog, right?"

I said this to my sawn-off Japanese shotgun before standing resolutely, rolling up my pants and laughing at my legs, strong, balanced and hairy (which Grandma told me means strength). I looked into the waters: bonnie grey eyes smiled back, a thatch of hair blazed with sunlight and the childish face of Kornyi Dizik stared back.

I waved my fist at him and glimpsed the stork's tracks.

I must go! But breakfast wouldn't hurt, eh?

But I remembered that, when a soldier saw a green shirt in the village, they aimed carefully, as at a dead willow, and yelled, shooting in fear, "Stop, you are not from here!"

This happened very rarely, for we deserters are fighting folk and move carefully, especially at dusk. The village is ours then and in the morning we pass through the rye. I decided not to breakfast; is it really okay to take a morsel to your mouth before mass?

I tugged the bunched hay, scuffed it with my feet (covering my tracks), examined my gun carefully, tucked it into my waistband, pulled my cap over my eyes and followed the stork's trail into the rye.

I didn't walk so much as swim because I wasn't lulled into the monotonous rhythm of the crops and the steppe was as friendly to me as my Japanese shortie, rousing me at dawn, summoning with its waves at midday and in the evening as the rye rose, falling asleep.

I followed familiar paths: wide Rozdil village welcomed with wheat, Temnyk greeted me with rye and the Hordyna burial mound wore a skirt of oats, barley and drunken buckwheat striped with blue flax flowers.

Everything was simple and clear, then suddenly dust rose from the steppe path, why?

I laid down my gun, looked askance at the track, my nerves accepted the song of the field seemingly singing along: a bee's wings buzzed above my ears irritatingly and I desperately wanted to squash it...

I looked more intently at the dusty trail, cavalry, cavalry, a thought sparks and is extinguished in blue flax, kill two, three then what will be... shooting yourself.

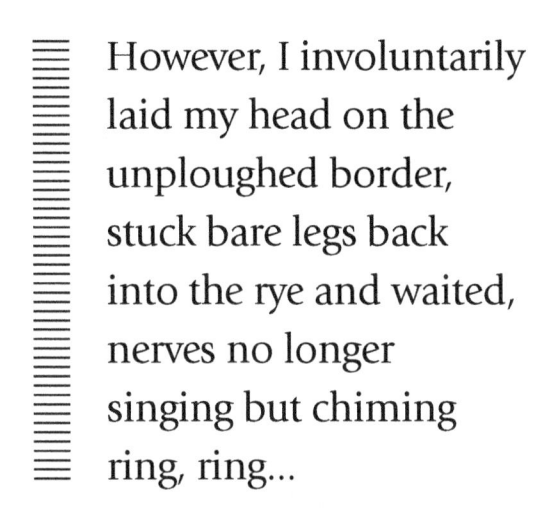

> However, I involuntarily laid my head on the unploughed border, stuck bare legs back into the rye and waited, nerves no longer singing but chiming ring, ring...

However, I involuntarily laid my head on the unploughed border, stuck bare legs back into the rye and waited, nerves no longer singing but chiming ring, ring...

Hooves burn beneath the sun, the rich man comes

Dzyuba, a wealthy guy from Hnylyshche, rode half a league away and halted his grey horse. The rye bore his loud, somewhat stilted conversation to me:

"Oh Brother! Zhytomyr province is full of those who won't serve in the commune but want easy bread."

Another guy who was on a wagon replied: "They all want to be commissars."

"Commissars! Let them be the devil! At night they're by the window with a rifle 'hand it over!'"

The grey strip of sand, the white hoof of the horse and my unconquered yearning to open fire lay behind them but I remembered Otaman Hostryi's order: "don't emerge and don't shoot."

I looked at a sinewy yarrow by the unploughed strip where a bee, legs caught in honeydew, thrashed, then smiled and climbed into the thick flax.

Let it be so.

Ring. Dzyuba. Ring. This bell rang the steppe to dinner. I was stressed from hunger and to →

But here she was now a wild steppe fruit tree, seared, tanned by the sun, her eyes two beetles

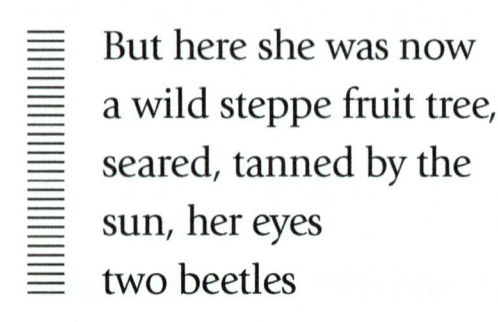

→ calm down I thought about Dzyuba.

He's probably had a good breakfast? You think that of the hero who found himself saying, "they want to be commissars." And although they would be commissars? No you can't say that to Hostryi. He would kill…

The ghost of the communist Matvyi Kiyanchuk, who was shot in Dzyuba's grounds, passed before me through the rye and my heart ached.

Ring.
On the barrel I sit
Beneath the barrel a duck
My bloke is a Bolshevik
And I, a *Haidamachka*

And he winked! Matvyi was a good lad, as they led him away

Ring.

I don't think about commissars, Hostryi might take me at night to bathe in the waters but still I wondered, who are they?

The steppe met the fragrant wind bowing low as it passed through the fields, warm and gentle it tugged whiskers of proud wheat, winked at oats and kissed, long, long, the curled heads of buckwheat. Drank the steppe honey.

I shook my head at it, I don't know, I wanted to think about Kiyanchuk but willed myself to stand up before sinking again because the wind fluttered a red kerchief above the road (the kerchief was all I saw from my lair): tassels like cranberry bunches touched ears of corn.

I'd spit on Hostryi now! I'll go meet 'em, maybe they'll even give me *pirozhki* although I'm not from "our village"… everything is possible for a deserter. Oh, curl-headed lass! Oh she's scared…

Sunday greetings where are you going? I didn't say but only thought is it Ulyana?

I pushed my cap back in surprise, what'd happen next?

It really was Ulyana in front of me, and along with her in my imagination stood the local lord's barn, six oxen harnessed to a plough how they turned the steppe soil once…

But here she was now like a wild steppe fruit tree, seared, tanned by the sun, her eyes two beetles. She carried water.

"Hello!" She came over to me.

"Good health Ulyana!" I wanted to smile and couldn't: she looked at me for a long time, visibly pondering and when her eye fell on my torn knee where a ladybird calmly crawled she laughed bashfully, her lips quivering like a child's, a tear rolling unnoticed onto her plaited hair… her blue eyes asked:

Did you, Kornyi, forget the manger near Zoryan's black ox? … and when you kissed my eyes, laughing, showing me a star through a knothole saying "they resemble that, don't they, dearest Ulyana?"

I stretched out my hand but didn't know where to begin, and asked stupidly, "You are unrecognisable now, Ulyana…"

Her words fell quietly onto the road:

"I have changed."

I don't remember what happened next: she bustled, then rushed at me yelling hoarsely,

"What kind of enemies are we…? No, Kornyi, we don't need to be! Let's sit down."

I was intoxicated… I don't know what I asked, nor what she told me, but I only remember how rye swayed wildly, flax trembled with joy and the hot wind fell with its chest to the ground.

Ears of grain listened.

"You are still handsome Kornyi… Do you want to kiss me? Kiss me, let at least one day be ours!"

She stroked my hair which had been combed two years running by rains, snows and the wolfish deserter lifestyle…

"Do you know my Dzyuba?" she laughed, "his name may mean beak but you are the devil's teeth!"

I laid my head in her lap listening, because she was my destiny, lost in the rye.

"Someone asked me this as if it were a song: mum only had to have three sons and three daughters…"

I was afraid of weeping and drunkenly asked:

"Is it true the rye ripens? But my lot will soon have to flee to the forest. There is the aristocratic life while we are starved as dogs and have to rob. The day passes while you wait for death. Do you have many comrades?"

"Oh, Kornyi! …ripening… Stop, you're crazy, don't go!"

I saw beautifully embroidered lace on the slender hems of Ulyana's garments, a maple leaf on her breast, and everything around was intoxicated, and the red kerchief caught fire and burned the steppe from end to end!

"Dearest Ulyana.. I'm not afraid of anything now!"

My dear little Ulyana…

Ears of corn whispered, she tugged her apron shyly, threw some small apricots to me and, with a quiet, timid sadness, said:

"I'll go to my mother's. He went to the council and is now their hostage, also they won't let people go anywhere…"

I delayed Ulyana by asking for the 20th or maybe last time, or perhaps I asked the maple leaf:

"Do you still love me?"

The flax blinked.

I don't know what I asked, nor what she told me, but I only remember how rye swayed wildly, flax trembled with joy and the hot wind fell with its chest to the ground

"Oh, that's so tactless even to ask," she paused and added, "eat the apricot, then we'll say goodbye." She kissed me quietly, tore up a handful of flax, and her eyes were blue, blue, as its flower and the fire of the kerchief faded.

"Goodbye, Kornyi!"

Then she raised her eyebrow in her old manner, blinked and laughed.

The rye ripens… no more is needed, goodbye! She bowed low on the track and rolled away with the green oat grass into a cheerful Chornoslyvka village and her mother's place.

Ding… oh ring out, steppe! I lay for a long time and listened to my heart ringing in time with the bells of the steppe. The ladybird crawled higher, I took it gently in my hand and asked: "Do you want to kneel, facing the sun?"

You can. Yes, grab your pants with your paws, then… stupid, you've fallen off. And how do you think I'm holding up? But, Ladybird, you don't know, that I, Kornyi Dizik, am drunk in the rye today, ha? You drunken rye grass, stand up! Spit on the death of Hostryi, I want to sing, do you hear, steppe?!

Oh, what kind of crow is that…

Hordyna's burial mound still burns with sunshine before me, it is Ulyana's red scarf and I… when I remember my deserter's life…

Are you asking about the communist Matvyi Kiyanchuk? I'll tell you, but not now, because my destiny is lost in the rye, and I want to cry like a child, or sing, as old people sing when they remember their youth. And keep singing. ✖

Hryhorii Kosynka (1899 -1934) was the Ukrainian author of several books. He was a representative of the Executed Renaissance, a group of more than 300 poets, writers and artists killed by the Soviet regime in the 1920s and 1930s

Notes: 1) Levadas are green watery areas in Ukraine. 2) A Haidamachka is a woman peasant rebel. 3) Pirozhki are fried yeast-leavened boat-shaped buns with a variety of fillings.

A life in exile

MACKENZIE ARGENT talks to Belarusian dissident **JANA PALIASHCHUK** about turning lemons to lemonade through her poetry

FOR 30 YEARS, Belarus has suffered under the rule of "Europe's last dictator", Alyaksandr Lukashenka. Many Belarusians have never known life outside of his regime, and with reports of voter suppression and Russian interference in elections earlier this year, the upcoming January 2025 presidential poll offers little hope of anything different. Public criticism of Lukashenka or his government is met with censorship, imprisonment and state violence. Many of those who refuse to hold their tongues have left Belarus.

Jana Paliashchuk is one such dissident. A Belarusian journalist, activist and poet who was vocal about the country's oppression and human rights violations, she fled following the disputed August 2020 presidential elections – the start of a persecution campaign against Belarusian journalists. Having previously worked in the office of opposition candidate Sviatlana

CULTURE

LEFT-TO-RIGHT: The cornflower is the national symbol of Belarus; a piece of the Berlin Wall in Potsdamer Platz, Berlin, engraved with support for Belarusian freedom; a protest against Lukashenka's regime in Minsk

Tsikhanouskaya, staying in Belarus was untenable. But leaving has not offered much respite.

"Many people do not feel safe living in Belarus, or even coming to Belarus, and lots of people are forced into exile," she told Index. "Some people, especially those who are not participating in activism, they've managed to settle down, to find a new life in exile, but I cannot find peace in this situation. I'm always reading the news. I'm always involved in events or campaigns."

She continued: "There's still pain every day, because every day something's happening. Somebody's relative is detained, or you're thinking about how your public work as an activist can affect your relatives staying in Belarus, especially as journalists. Since September 2020 there hasn't been a day where I didn't think about Belarus."

Being forced to leave her home country has made her feel as if a part of herself is missing. She said: "Once you live this, you understand that it's about small things: missing bread from your favourite bakery in Minsk, missing the streets where you went to school or university, where you walked all the time, missing the smell of chestnut trees in spring… it's in your DNA, it's who you are.

"My parents built a house on the land my great-grandfather had for many years. It's where they lived their lives, they had a garden, they raised their kids there, so it's a special place with which you have a connection.

"This house, where your mother grows roses, or where you have strawberries in the summer, you just miss it; you feel disconnected from something as big as Belarus, and you feel disconnected from something as small as this house. It's a disconnection on every level."

Paliashchuk started writing poetry in 2019 about a past relationship – but now, she's writing about her strained relationship with her country, in the hope that her work can help people understand how it feels to be in exile.

"I feel really blessed that I have these tools to transform something painful into something beautiful, into art…" she said. "We have these lemons and now we have to make lemonade. We cannot come and destroy Lukashenka's regime, but at least we can do something about the pain he's causing."

Mackenzie Argent is editorial assistant at Index

CREDIT: Jana Paliashchuk

I feel blessed that I have tools to transform something painful into something beautiful

53(04):104/106|DOI:10.1177/03064220241306641

INDEXONCENSORSHIP.ORG **105**

Courage

Courage
Is such a predictable word
To describe
People
Struggling hard
To own their country
Yet – does one really know
What courage is?

Courage is
Watching them straight in the eye
Knowing
They're eager for you
To taste their batons

Courage is
Being loud
Knowing that nobody
Cares to listen

Courage is
Piercing your throat with a pen
Being caged like an animal
Not piercing
Is also courage

Courage is
Smiling
When a gavel bangs loudly
With no more mercy
Than a guillotine has
Sentencing to not seeing sunlight
For two more years
Or twelve
It's all the same for them

Courage is
Going outside
After 30 years
Of the same outcome

Their boots taste like your blood
And the blood of your parents

Home

My legs wobble

Have been since I walked out
Of my land

From that day,
I constantly lose
Any ground beneath my feet

They sold our soil
To the horrible people

I would crawl back
I would lay my bones there
Yet I'm forced to carry them
To unknown borders
Like the stranger I am

Step by step
Day by day
I trip and I tremble
Lost any remnants of peace

And even in my sleep
My legs wobble
Have been
Since I walked out of my land
And became an
Outlander

Home-sick

I hate the colour of window frames
My parents chose for our
New family house

Sometimes, I just forget
I'll never see them
Anyway ✖

Jana Paliashchuk is a Belarusian poet, activist and communications specialist in exile. She is a researcher on Index's Letters from Lukashenka's Prisoners project

An unfathomable tragedy

SARAH DAWOOD introduces **DIMI REIDER**'s piece of prose written on 7 October 2024 to mark 12 months of devastation in the Middle East

ABOVE: Palestinians inspect the site of an Israeli strike on tents of displaced people in Deir Al-Balah, the central Gaza Strip in November 2024

IT'S BEEN MORE than a year since Hamas's brutal incursion into Israel on 7 October, when the militant group killed 1,200 people and took more than 250 people hostage. It was the deadliest day for Jewish people since the Holocaust. In response, Israel launched a devastating war on Gaza that has caused, and continues to cause, immense suffering and destruction. Benjamin Netanyahu's government has killed nearly 44,000 Palestinians, including at least 14,000 children.

There has also been an assault on free speech and the press. According to the Committee to Protect Journalists (CPJ), this has been the most lethal conflict for journalists since 1992, claiming the lives of at least 137 media workers (overwhelmingly Palestinian), at least five of whom were directly targeted by Israeli forces.

The war has since expanded to Lebanon, where Israel has gone on the offensive against Hezbollah and more than 3,200 people have been killed. Meanwhile there have been back-and-forth missile attacks with Iran. Serious concerns remain worldwide that the situation could escalate into a full-blown regional war. A recent ceasefire deal agreed between Hezbollah and Israel offers a small glimmer of hope that an end to the fighting could be in sight – though when, we do not know.

Amidst the human devastation, displacement and death, social media has proven itself to be at once a tool for fearless reportage and propaganda, for free speech and silencing. When international news crews were banned from entering conflict zones, brave on-the-ground Palestinian reporters risked their lives to share videos and testimonies online to show the world the truth. Yet social media has also been a cataclysmic playground for vitriol.

Exactly one year on from 7 October 2023, London-based Israeli journalist Dimi Reider reflected on the suffering of both Palestinians and Israelis in this short piece of prose reprinted below. He originally wrote it for Elon Musk's platform X, which has been rife with hatred targeted at both Jewish and Muslim communities, Israelis and Palestinians, often by those with no connection to the conflict.

He reflects on the binary, "us-versus-them" culture that has propagated online in self-righteous, tit-for-tat echo chambers, whilst those in Gaza, Israel and Lebanon, and their loved ones elsewhere, are forever scarred by the horrific brutality of the past year.

Sarah Dawood is editor at Index

CREDIT: Imago / Omar Ashtawy / Alamy

One endless day, and what comes after

By Dimi Reider

I THOUGHT I'D be writing a big analytical piece on the anniversary of 7 October. Where we've been, where we're going. What I got wrong, who got what right. And maybe I'll write some of this yet.

But in truth, it doesn't feel like the day for it. Not only because I don't want to add to the cloud of analysis on a day so many people, from every side, are coming up here to share their own personal pain. But mainly because it doesn't feel like an anniversary. Anniversaries imply revisiting an event defined in time: a death, a marriage, a birth, the establishment of a state, the publication of a book, the inauguration of something, the ceremonial end of something else.

None of this applies: 7 October never ended, and not just because Israeli TV seems to eternally return to the stories of that one day at the expense of so many other stories. 7 October never ended because it became 8 October and 10 October and 12 October, and then we killed Refaat, who loathed the Israeli state but taught Hebrew poetry to his students in Gaza; and Vivian's body was found and "missing" was augmented to "dead" over and over again, and children were blasted apart, so many children, and we may or may not have torched that first hospital but we've flattened so many more since, and so many hearts broke, and broke again, and broke again, or cracked, or hardened, or simply stopped. And we killed hostages, and they killed hostages, and in the midst of it all, one hostage, an older woman, on her way home, stopped before one of her captors, and bid him farewell, and the world saw his hand come off the trigger of his assault rifle to reach out and shake hers.

And then we went right back to it, and it got worse, and worse again, and we graduated from disproportionate violence to genocidal almost seamlessly because most genocides snowball from tiny decisions and from impunity, not from a flowchart in a letterhead notepaper in a villa by a lake; and every red line any of us ever imagined turned out just that - imaginary: because it turns out that yes, people who've been through horrible things, or feel like they've been through horrible things will do horrible things, and film themselves doing it, and make stupid jokes about doing it, and then do them again, all the while feeling like they're the victims; and no one should be surprised because no one is, in fact, under an obligation to become a better or more forgiving person because of their trauma.

And meanwhile, folks on, say, Twitter, will piss all over the graves of yours or somebody else's loved ones, excuse or shrug off every atrocity, and then imagine atrocities not yet committed and loudly luxuriate in wishing those on people they never met, their fists pounding their keyboards, their teeth chattering even if their jaws are clenched or stretched in a rictus grin – because alongside the rage everyone is afraid, or afraid of being afraid, or afraid of seeing each other or seeing each other in each other; and behind the clatter of the keys, there is a thin, almost constant, almost silent scream: WHY CAN'T YOU SEE ME and HOW DARE YOU NOT SEE ME and HOW DARE ANYONE SEE YOU WHEN THEY SHOULD SEE ME, or, somewhat more sanely, can't they please, please, see me, for a change. See us.

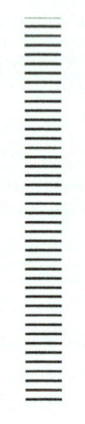

> People who've been through horrible things, or feel like they've been through horrible things, will do horrible things, and film themselves doing it

And it's still going on, expanding, corroding every bit of the land, and now it's in Lebanon and in Syria and in Yemen and perhaps even soon in Iran, and it's poisoning even distant democracies, and the same politicians are still making the same excuses – yes, the same politicians; because incredibly, or all too credibly, not one person directly responsible has lost their job (except by assassination, which really isn't good enough.) It's 7 Oct v. 366, and Sinwar is still here, and Biden's still here, and, God help us, even Netanyahu's still here, now and for the foreseeable.

And so are we.

And it is this, quite simply, which gives me – not so much hope, which can make for a dangerous medicine, but rather the plain knowledge of perseverance. We are still here, Palestinians and Israelis, clenching our homeland or stretching to it from great distance. Still here.

(I don't for a minute take this for granted; I was fairly sure, for example, that all surviving Gazans would be pushed out to Egypt within the first quarter; this hasn't happened yet, and I'm almost sure that it won't; among the great cruelty, a small, bitter mercy.)

We are still here, and among the great rending there are countless stitches that hold – tying us to the land and to each other: in part thanks to people managing to stay human, in part thanks to very hard, unglamorous small-scale mediation work, we have not yet become Rwanda.

And there are new stitches being made every day. New dialogue groups open and instantly get oversubscribed. New projects, single-identity and cross-community, are being thought up, organised, put into play. New ideas, sidestepping or venturing far, far beyond a reheated Oslo process; new alliances, new ideas, new vocabularies, new modes of being together and being apart, new ways of thinking about each other even for those who aren't talking to each other yet. The Palestinian liberation movement is rejuvenating and rebuilding. Israelis you would never expect to be taking on the toughest challenges and questions, or to give radically new

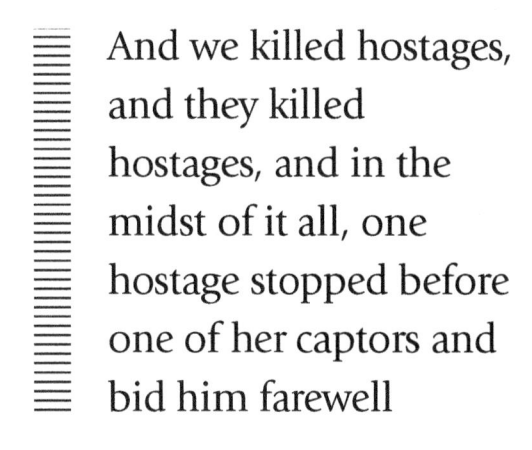

> And we killed hostages, and they killed hostages, and in the midst of it all, one hostage stopped before one of her captors and bid him farewell

answers, are doing just that.

There's a lot going on. Anaemic? Bit dull? Bit flat? Not as evocative as the horrors I listed earlier? Perhaps. We are generally not wired towards things like community work, mediation, deconfliction; you don't need adrenaline pumping and heart racing and every nerve in your body engaged to draw lines on a flip chart or sit in a room for the 30th time trying to catch the subtlest change in tone or in language that hints at a possible opening to change. But this, too, is the work that needs doing and it is being done, on scales more grand and more granular than many of us might imagine.

So yes. It's 7 October, the 366th of this war. Year 95, if that's how you count, of the conflict. Year 76 of the Nakba and of the Jewish state. And the work goes on. Because even if we aren't there yet, there is an "after" to the now. And we're still here, and there is much good work worth doing – some now, some being prepared for later, some being written for much, much later on.

What more can one say. Condolences to those grieving in ways I can't even conceive of. ✖

Dimi Reider is an Israeli journalist based in London and has a background in conflict mediation. He is national editor at The Lead and co-founder of +972 magazine, and has written for The New York Times, Haaretz, the London Review of Books and Index on Censorship

You are now free

Exile from Sudan has not silenced novelist **ABDELAZIZ BARAKA SAKIN**, whose words are now being shared in English – including this exclusive translation for Index. **KATIE DANCEY-DOWNS** introduces his work

ABOVE: Abdelaziz Baraka Sakin was forced into exile in 2012

SUDANESE AUTHOR ABDELAZIZ Baraka Sakin knows a thing or two about book bans. While his first collection of short stories was welcomed and published by the Sudanese Ministry of Culture in 2005 under president Omar al-Bashir's regime, later that year it was banned by that same ministry. He then had the unhappy honour of his book, The Jungo, adding fuel to what he believes to be the country's first book burning in 2010. And in 2012, his books were confiscated from the Khartoum International Book Fair, after which he was arrested and detained.

In that same year, he went into exile in Europe, his stories about Africa now written from Austria and France. In 2020 he was awarded the Prix de la Littérature Arabe (Arab Literature Prize), and in 2023 he was ordained as a Knight of the Order of Arts and Letters for contributions to literature in France, proving that exile has not silenced him.

Today, most of Sakin's works are banned in his home country. He has previously said that this is down to his writings about his own Nubian culture, which fall short of the government's narrative of what it means to be Sudanese. And yet his books are secretly traded and circulated among Sudanese readers, making him one of the country's most popular writers.

When al-Bashir was overthrown by the military in 2019, Sakin still did not feel safe returning to Sudan. He stands against the "military dictatorship", as he described it to the Austrian outlet Kleine Zeitung.

Until now, his work has not been available in English. So it is with much celebration that Mayada Ibrahim and Adil Babikir's translation of the Arabic-language *Samahani*, which is Swahili for "forgive me", is now available in the UK through Foundry Editions. There is less to celebrate in Oman and Kuwait however, where the book is banned.

The novel is set in 19th century Zanzibar and explores the relationship between a powerful Omani princess and her eunuch African slave, who was captured and castrated by Arab slavers. The story comes from Sakin's own experiences of displacement and exile, and is described as a "furious cry against persecution in all its forms".

With his first novel-in-translation now available in English, Sakin gave Index the opportunity to publish one of his Arabic short stories, Hallucination, in English for the first time. Consider this another text for the underground reading circles.

Katie Dancey-Downs is assistant editor at Index

≡ Go ahead, all chains are broken.
Unleash your imagination

CREDIT: Midas PR

Hallucination

By **ABDELAZIZ BARAKA SAKIN**

YES, WRITE WHATEVER you want, in any language, with any phrases, in any style, about anything. Your grandmother Virginia Woolf said: "All topics are fit for writing."

Write about humanity, freedom, sex, politics, religion, homeland, women… yes, women, the myth of creation and the miracle of the creator, the guide of the unbelieving atheist to God. Write about her, say she is beautiful, enchanting, desired, wicked, magnificent, corrupt and sacred, a prophetess, and pure. Sculpt her body, paint her, colour her chest with sand or with seawater if you wish.

Write about the soul, love, betrayal, war, language, the ruler, the ruled, Noam Chomsky, Karl Marx, dictatorship, democracy, oil, war, Judas Iscariot, God, Salman Rushdie. Write "The Satanic Verses", go ahead… Let loose.

The pens and papers are ready for you. The printing presses are waiting. Those brushes, oils and acrylics, all materials of the earth are subjects for painting. Paint, sculpt, colour, piss if you want in the face of history. Criticise. Be Victor Jara, Henri Matisse, al-Salih, Paul Klee, Sheikh Imam, Mostafa Sid Ahmed, Nâzim Hikmet, Muzaffar al-Nawab, Abdullah Didan, Ahmed Matar, Mayakovsky, Mahmoud Mohammed Taha. Be yourselves, as Buddha says.

Write rebellious plays, damned blasphemous poetry like Rania Mahjoub's, beautiful music, films, songs, unclassifiable prose, whatever you want, I mean whatever you desire. Damn it, all censorship has been lifted, the security officers, monitors, spies and guardians of intentions have been dismissed. The members of the reviewing committees, the text approval councils, the censorship boards have been sent to the furnace of history, never to return.

You are now free: writers and novelists, painters, al-Noor Osman Abkar, Mai al-Tijani, singers, composers, gravediggers, tailors.

Go ahead, all chains are broken. Unleash your imagination, create as long as you were made for it. It is both my personal and professional responsibility, and the responsibility of the state. ✖

*Translated by **Hossam Fazulla***

LAST WORD

Putin will not stop until he's stopped

The winner of the Trustees Award at the 2024 Freedom of Expression Awards talks to Index about her campaigning

EVGENIA KARA-MURZA NEVER expected to become an activist but in 2023, when her husband – anti-war protester and journalist Vladimir Kara-Murza – was sentenced to 25 years in a Russian prison, she campaigned tirelessly for his release and for the principles he stood for.

He was kept in a high-security prison in solitary confinement after his detention, but one day last August he was woken at three in the morning.

"At that moment, I was absolutely certain that I was being led out to be executed," he told the BBC.

In fact, the early wake-up was part of a huge prisoner swap between Russia and Western countries which saw him freed in a deal brokered by Turkey.

Evgenia Kara-Murza, who has been named as the winner of the Trustees Award at the 2024 Freedom of Expression Awards, spoke to Index about her husband's detention, her campaigning and her vision of the future.

INDEX How did you become an activist?

EVGENIA KARA-MURZA I do not particularly enjoy the public character of my work but, with the criminal invasion of Ukraine and repression in Russia, I believe it is my responsibility as a Russian citizen to do what I can to stop this evil.

INDEX How do you feel about the prisoner swap?

EVGENIA KARA-MURZA On a personal level it all still feels quite surreal. What I think is important to emphasise, though, is the symbolic significance of Russian political prisoners being included in the swap. Thus, Western governments sent a clear message to the Kremlin that they fully realise who the real criminals are and that they think it important to stand with and to fight for the lives of those Russians who are being persecuted.

INDEX Do you think the West needs to do more to oppose Putin?

EVGENIA KARA-MURZA The invasion of Ukraine and widespread repression in Russia are the results of more than two decades of impunity when Western governments, at different times and for different reasons, continuously appeased the dictator by offering him compromises and disregarding gross human rights violations. The free world needs to realise that Putin will not stop until he is stopped – and act accordingly.

INDEX Do you think you and your husband will be able to return?

EVGENIA KARA-MURZA I am absolutely convinced that Vladimir will be one of those who, following the collapse of the regime, will roll up his sleeves to contribute to the rebuilding of the country from scratch and turn it into a functioning democracy.

INDEX If you were detained in prison, which book would you take with you?

EVGENIA KARA-MURZA Choosing a single one would be difficult. My family knows that I cannot go by a bookstore without peeking in – if only to touch book spines.

INDEX Which news headline would you like to see?

EVGENIA KARA-MURZA "The recent parliamentary election in Russia, the first held in the post-Putin era, has been declared free and fair by international observers."

INDEX What is the future for Russia?

EVGENIA KARA-MURZA Russia in its current state will always be a threat to itself and everyone around, and the only true guarantee of peace and stability on the European continent is a democratic Russia. Millions of people in Russia want their country to be free and peaceful. More than 1,000 people are already behind bars for publicly denouncing the Kremlin's aggressive policies, and new detentions and arrests are happening daily. These people represent the democratic alternative to the current regime, and the future of Russia greatly depends on whether Vladimir Putin is allowed to destroy this alternative. ✖

ABOVE: Evgenia Kara-Murza and her children talk on the phone to their husband and father, the detained journalist Vladimir Kara-Murza following a prisoner swap with Russia in August 2024.

CREDIT: Official White House Photo by Adam Schultz